Alan Coren was [...] leaving Oxford U[...] Commonwealth Fellowship to Yale and Berkeley. He returned to England in 1963 to become an assistant editor on *Punch*. He became editor of that magazine in 1977. He writes for radio, television and films and is a frequent broadcaster both in England and the United States. He has so far written ten books for adults, eight books for children and edited several anthologies.

Also by Alan Coren in Sphere Books:

TISSUES FOR MEN

The Cricklewood Diet

ALAN COREN

SPHERE BOOKS LIMITED
30–32 Gray's Inn Road, London WC1X 8JL

First published in Great Britain by
Robson Books Ltd 1982
Copyright © Alan Coren 1982
Published by Sphere Books Ltd 1983

The author would like to thank the proprietors of *Punch*
magazine for permission to reproduce material in
this book.

TRADE
MARK

Set in Baskerville

Printed and bound in Great Britain by
Cox & Wyman Ltd, Reading

Contents

Vorspeise

Unlike the prolegomena of my earlier works, this is no ordinary vorspeise. Hitherto, it has always been my practice to use this doodling-space to explain my title, if only to myself. This time, that function is beyond me: I do not know why this book is called *The Cricklewood Diet*.

All I know is that it is something to do with a great breakthrough in publishing. My publisher tells me that various clues have been scattered through this book, possibly in the form of typographical errors or lousy jokes, which he has himself inserted in the text. If I succeed in identifying all these and working out the complex pattern they can be made to form, they will constitute a solution to the Quest.

The Quest is for my royalty cheque, which has been buried somewhere in Southern England. I gather this is something which smart publishers do to get television coverage for otherwise unshiftable piles of books.

The title is thus the first of these clues. It does not necessarily mean that the money, such as it is, is buried in Cricklewood. Cricklewood could well be a red herring, tricky though that is to visualize. I tell you all this partly to apologise for a title which is going to embarrass your shelfspace, but mainly to enlist your help: if you get the clues before I do, give me a ring. The sooner I get the cheque, the sooner I can put an end to this nonsense and bring out a second edition with a sensible title which will leave nobody in any doubt whatever about what they're getting for their money.

When the time comes, *Moby Twist* is going to be really big.

AC

In the Beginning

A five-year computer analysis unveiled by the Haifa Technion has concluded that Genesis was written by a single hand. The head of the research team described his findings as a minor bombshell: the theory that had dominated biblical scholarship for a hundred years was that Genesis grew out of folk tales edited in the days of David. But who was the author? The professor would say no more than that single authorship strengthens the traditional claim of Moses. – The Guardian

Moses tweaked a sliver of manna from between his molars, and stared gloomily across the scrubby dunes.

'Eighteen years,' he murmured. 'This is some wilderness! This is, like, a really major nowhere. How did we ever get into this crazy deal?'

'Who knew?' said his brother Aaron. 'What did we know from wildernesses? Were we explorers? We were in the construction business. Pyramids, we know about.'

'Roads,' said Moses, 'we know about.'

'You want a sphinx,' said Aaron, 'we can quote you. But wildernesses? I remember thinking: we'll get out of Cairo, we'll walk maybe a mile or two, we'll find a good hotel, that's it.'

'Personally,' said Moses, 'I was hoping we'd get to America.'

Aaron looked at him.

'What the hell is America?' he enquired.

'I gather it's a terrific opportunity,' replied Moses. 'Especially if you have a good trade, for example the construction business. You can clean up.'

'They need pyramids in America?'

'Naturally they need pyramids, dummy! Who doesn't need pyramids? You die, you need a pyramid. Everybody dies.'

Aaron picked up a piece of lunch, blew the sand off carefully, chewed for a while, thinking. 'Who told you about this America?' he said, finally.

'I heard it from a bush,' said Moses.

Aaron, about to swallow, choked. His brother slapped his back.

'A *bush*?' cried Aaron, when he had recovered. 'We're here eighteen years on account of some bush told you about opportunities in the construction business? Who takes career advice from vegetation? What made you think it was telling the truth, anyhow?'

'It was burning,' said Moses. 'What did it have to gain by lying?'

Aaron looked over his shoulder, down from the dune towards the scorching wadi in which forty thousand people were mooning about disconsolately on the never-ending quest for new ways of cooking manna.

'They ever get to hear you brought them all this way on the recommendation of a plant,' he said, 'we're dead men.'

Moses shrugged.

'Nobody twisted their arms,' he said. 'They were sick of working for Egyptians, they wanted their own businesses, they left of their own accord, so how come suddenly I'm responsible? Also, you're forgetting the plagues, unless maybe you think the plagues are down to me as well?'

'Don't get agitated,' said Aaron.

'Normally, frogs start falling on people's heads, they come to their own conclusions about leaving the neighbourhood,' said Moses, heavily. 'Normally, you see everybody suddenly sprouting boils, you put your house on the market. Normally, you notice first-born going down like flies, you reckon this is not a great place to bring up kids.'

'Who's arguing?' said Aaron. 'I wonder why it all happened?'

'In a word,' replied Moses, 'prawns.'

'Prawns?'

Moses nodded.

'The things Egyptians eat, you wouldn't believe. No wonder they get boils. No wonder the kids die. Did you ever see a prawn? It's an insect. A normal person sees a prawn, he treads on it. With Egyptians, they grab a saucepan. When I get around to it, I'm going to draw up a list of things you shouldn't eat. Could be a big seller.'

'It still doesn't explain the hailstones,' countered Aaron.

'If they'd stayed indoors like us,' said Moses, 'they'd have been all right. As it was, my guess is they were all out looking for prawns. Bend over a puddle looking for a tasty insect, next thing, bang! A hailstone on the head.'

'Alternatively,' said a voice, 'a rock!'

The brothers looked up, startled. From behind a nearby cactus, three men emerged: their jaws were set, their eyes were narrowed, their hirsute forearms twanged with tensed sinew.

'What's this,' snarled the largest, 'about a bush?'

'I was a foreman,' said the second, 'I was pulling down a good screw, plus pension rights. Now I'm out here eighteen years on account of a talking shrub?'

'Correction,' snapped the third, 'what you are out here eighteen years on account of is a man with terminal craziness.'

'I didn't know craziness could kill you,' said the second.

'Sometimes,' said the first man, raising his rock, 'it needs a little help.'

'WAIT!' cried Moses. 'You think that was an ordinary bush? Ha! That was a god!'

The three hesitated.

'A *god*?' muttered the largest man. 'What kind of a god has leaves?'

'He is not,' said Moses, 'always a bush. Sometimes, he's a pillar of fire. Another day, could be a cloud.'

'A cloud?'

'Or a chair. A shoe. Anything. It all depends on the

circumstances.' Moses licked his lips. 'Look, if you don't believe me, how about that business with the Red Sea?'

'You mean where the equinoctial inflow moved against the current, due to the fact that the volume of the tidal wave was greater than the prevailing stream-volume, producing a temporary sharp drop in level?' said the largest man.

'Superstitious heathen claptrap!' cried Moses. 'That was the god, looking after his chosen people. Also,' here he brandished a piece of manna, 'what do you think of *this*?'

'Not a lot,' said the second man. 'Can he do steak?'

'Steak is just a load of cholesterol,' snapped Moses. 'You think he wants we should all get heart disease? This is one smart god, believe me!'

They looked at one another doubtfully; but they lowered their rocks.

'What's his name?' asked the largest man.

'His name is –' said Moses, and stopped. His brow creased. 'His name is –' His brow uncreased. 'It is forbidden,' he said, 'to utter his name! That'll give you some idea of how big he is.'

'Pick up the rocks,' said the largest man, to the other two.

'On the other hand,' said Moses, quickly, 'there are special circumstances. How much can it hurt? His name is – is Jehovah!'

The largest man stared at him.

'What kind of a name is that?' He turned to his companions. 'Does that sound godlike to you?'

'Jack would be better,' said the second man. 'Jack is a name you can trust. Sam, even.'

'What sort of people are you?' roared Moses, a little confidence restored. 'He brings the plagues down on the Gyppoes, he opens the Red Sea for you, he delivers groceries to the door, and you object to his *name*? Listen, I –'

'What bringing down the plagues?' objected the third

4

man. 'You said that was because we didn't eat prawns, I heard you!'

'Aha!' cried Moses. 'But what *stops* us from eating the prawns?'

'For me,' said the largest man, 'it's the little legs.'

'Plus how the eyes stick out,' said the second man.

'It was Jehovah!' shouted Moses. 'It's all in the book.'

'Book, what book?' said the third man.

'Never mind what book!' snapped Moses. 'Who are you, all of a sudden you want to know everything? All you have to do is believe, that's the way it is with gods, and if I tell you something, that's the way it is, who did the bush choose to speak to in the first place?'

The three considered this for a while. Aaron stared at the trembling line of the horizon, wishing he had something to pray to.

'All right,' said the largest man, at last. 'Suppose we go along with the plagues, the sea, the whole bit, just tell me this? How come he picked us for the ritzy treatment, leading us to where there was unparalleled opportunities for private building firms?'

Moses cleared his throat. 'That,' he said, 'is – that is on account of he is the God of the Construction Business!'

'Are you serious?'

'Definitely. Like with the Egyptians where they have a God of Fertility, a God of Hunting, a God of This, a God of That, so what we got, naturally, was the God of the Construction Business. Better yet, that is absolutely the top god there is! He built the whole damn thing!'

'What whole damn thing?' enquired the third man.

'The world, dummy!' cried Moses. 'It was his idea, before he came up with it, there was nothing. A hole. In –' Moses paused, but only momentarily '– in six days! To include making good.'

'*Six days?*' exclaimed the largest man. 'For a *world*? It could take that long to order the nails.'

'He's a god!' shouted Moses. 'You think he has to hang around waiting for planning permission? He wants a world, he builds a world!' He wiped a sleeve across his gleaming forehead. 'Anyway, it's all in the book.'

'Again he mentioned the book,' remarked the second man.

'So show us the book,' demanded the largest man.

Moses grabbed Aaron's arm.

'Show them the book!' he muttered.

'Me?' cried Aaron. 'You want *me* to show them the book?'

'You mean,' said Moses, 'you haven't *got* the book?'

'That's right,' said Aaron, glaring at him. 'I haven't got the book.'

Moses turned to the three men, shaking his head, smiling.

'How do you like that?' he said. 'Somebody must have borrowed the book. Isn't it incredible the way people are with books, they take them off the shelves, they say this looks pretty good, mind if I borrow it, you say sure, take it, but do you ever see it again?'

The three men looked at one another, and twitched their cloaks.

'You got six hours to find the book,' said the largest man.

They walked out of sight into the wadi.

'That was pretty quick thinking, back there with the bush and the god and everything,' said Aaron.

'Leadership,' said Moses, 'is about not panicking in emergencies.'

'Also,' said Aaron, 'it's about coming up with a book in around six hours.'

'Yes,' said Moses, 'it's about that, too. Tell me, you got any papyrus in there?'

Aaron unslung his goatskin scrip, and rummaged.

'Papyrus I got,' he replied, 'also a stylus. What I haven't got is ideas.'

Moses shrugged.

'What ideas?' he said. 'You spend a couple of pages setting the scene then right away, boom! You bring on a couple of naked people, they fool around a bit, then

6

there's a murder, that's the kind of thing people go for, then some disaster stuff, a conflagration, maybe, a flood, something like that – I tell you, there's forty thousand people down there, they had nothing to do for eighteen years, they're gonna fall on this like – like manna from, er, from wherever manna comes from. I tell you, this book is going to be very big! I'll dictate, you write.' He cleared his throat. *'In the beginning –'*

'Hold on!' said Aaron. 'What's wrong with *Once upon a time*?'

Moses snorted.

'Are you crazy?' he said. 'You want it to sound like a fairy story?'

Biggles
Strikes
Camp

Daily Mirror

The shattering roar of the engine was bad, but the heat was worse. Trapped in the juddering seat, the whirling blades inches from his head and howling on maximum revs, Biggles wondered whether something might not have gone terribly wrong. He tried to turn, but the restriction of that tiny space prevented him from seeing Algy behind him. He could hear Algy shouting something, but he could not, in the fearful din and the rushing of the air, make out the words. Desperately, Biggles waved a hand, hoping against hope that Flight-Lieutenant the Hon. Algernon Lacy, with whom he had been through so much, would draw on that long partnership now and interpret his brief signal correctly.

Algy did not fail him. A switch was flicked, the motor cut out, the roaring died, and with it the vibration and the dreadful heat. It was over!

Squadron-Leader James Bigglesworth, DSO, drew a deep breath, and slid out from beneath the hair-drier.

'What was all that shrieking about, you silly mare?' he enquired.

'I suddenly remembered about the conditioner,' said Algy. 'I suddenly said to myself, oh my *Gawd*, I said, I never put any hair conditioner on her, she'll frizzle up like nobody's business, I said, you know what *her* ends go like after a day in an open cockpit!'

Biggles leapt to his feet, shot his trusty co-pilot one of his most withering Looks, and ran over to the mess mirror. He took one glance, and screamed faintly.

'I look like Greer Garson!' he cried. 'It's flying all over everywhere! It's very fine, my hair, it's always been fine,

8

body is what it lacks, it lacks *body*, I don't know how many times I've told you about not forgetting the conditioner, I remember the night we were over Bremen and that silly old queen Hopcroft caught a tracer bullet in his head and I was *covered* in icky blood and brains and everything, I remember saying to you *then*, I said I've just had this streak put in and now it's *soaked*, I'll have to rinse it out in lemon juice, and you threw one of your fits and said where are we going to get lemon juice, don't you know there's a war on, and I said never mind that, just remember *after* the lemon juice you'll have to put lots and lots of conditioner on, otherwise . . .'

'You don't half go on,' muttered Algy. 'I've only got one pair of hands, I can't be bloody everywhere, I had to comb out Gimlet's perm in the middle of everything.'

'It looks ever so nice,' said Gimlet, from the other side of the mess, examining the moustache in a little mother-of-pearl pocket-mirror. 'It's come up exactly parallel, Algy. I think I look like Ward Bond. Do *you* think I look like Ward Bond, Skip?'

Biggles glared at his navigator.

'*Skip?*' he mimicked, dropping his voice an octave. 'Ward Bond? Our little friend would appear to be feeling very masculine this morning, Algy. What do you suppose has come over him, if you'll pardon the expression?'

Algy removed the Kirby grips from his mouth.

'I blame that hormone cream she uses on her legs,' he said. 'Start with that, you never know where it's going to end. Personally, give me a good pluck every time.'

Biggles nodded.

'She thinks she looks like Ward Bond,' he said. 'If you want my opinion, dear, I'd say it was more like Anne Baxter tucking into a piece of shredded wheat!'

Algy shrieked, and fell against his captain. They foxtrotted briefly, and when they broke apart again, breathless, Gimlet had gone, slamming the hardboard door.

'Temper!' shouted Biggles. He sat down, and his co-pilot began skilfully to comb him out. Biggles, soothed, closed his eyes; but at the tap on the door, they snapped open again. 'That'll be Gimlet back to say she's sorry,' he said confidently. 'I can read her like a *book*!'

'Be firm,' murmured Algy, the tail-comb flicking.

But it was not the trusty Gimlet who strode into the mess. It was a tall, slim, freckled, red-headed youth, who saluted formally, and then, shyly, grinned.

'Who's this?' said Biggles.

'Call me Ginger,' said the youth, 'everybody does.'

'Yes, well, they would, wouldn't they, dear?' said Biggles. 'What can we do for you, if it isn't a silly answer?'

'Gimlet has told the Wing-Commander that he's not going to fly with you any more,' said Ginger, 'so I've been assigned to your crew instead.'

Biggles sprang from the chair. *Vogue* slid from his lap.

'*You?*' he screamed. '*You*, fly with *us*?'

Ginger's soft face fell. His lower lip trembled.

'Why not?' he enquired.

Biggles grabbed him by the arm, and dragged both him and Algy to the mirror.

'Look!' he cried. 'Algy's brunette, I'm ash-blonde, and you're a redhead! We look like the Andrews Sisters! It's such bad *taste*!'

'You don't *have* to be blonde,' murmured Algy. 'I could put a nice tawny tint on it. Or you could wear a wig.'

Biggles reeled!

'Me? A *wig*? Gumming it on like some poor old poof behind the scout hut, before going out to paste Jerry over the Ruhr, is that what you think this war is all about?'

'I think it's a super idea!' cried Ginger, clapping his hands. 'If you got shot down and it flew off and you were captured, the RAF could drop a spare into the camp, just like Douglas Bader!'

Algy giggled, and clapped him on the shoulder, gently.

'I think I'm going to like you,' he said. 'By the way, we

10

haven't been introduced, I'm –'

'You have to be the faithful Algy,' said Ginger, offering his hand.

Algy held it.

'No *have to* about it, dear,' he murmured.

'I'll kill you!' hissed Biggles.

There is no telling what might have happened then, if the klaxon had not clanged, summoning them to the morning's briefing. Ginger and Algy instantly snatched up their flight-pads and teddies and ran; Biggles, caught in indecision between his pastel-blue flying scarf and the cerise with the polka-dots, followed on. When he arrived at the briefing hut, it was already full, and buzzing with excited gossip, in which Biggles had no chance to join, for at that very moment the door to the left of the dais opened, and the impressive figure of the Group-Captain limped in, followed, as always, by the loyal and almost equally impressive figure of his trusty cat, Bosie.

'He's so, oooh, I don't know,' murmured Algy. 'Very few people can get away with a game leg.'

'*You* could, Algy,' whispered Ginger. 'You've got the presence.'

Biggles hit him with his flight-bag. Sequins flew. Men went *shoosh!*

'Right, chaps,' bellowed the Group-Captain, taking a corner of the green baize that hung down over the blackboard, 'shan't keep you in suspense!'

He flung back the cloth.

The hut, as one man, gasped!

Pinned to the blackboard was a detailed drawing of the mess, covered in multi-coloured squiggles. Here and there, swatches of cloth dangled from pins, with paint-charts beside them.

'It's the new wallpaper and curtains!' breathed Algy.

The Group-Captain tapped the board with his pointer.

'Now,' he said, 'I've had a word with our chums the boffins, and they tell me that if we want an apricot dado, there is –'

11

'PELMETS?' thundered a voice.

The men swivelled, craned. The Group-Captain's face darkened.

'There will be an opportunity for questions later, Bigglesworth,' he said. 'Meanwhile, if you would be so –'

'They went out with the *ark*, pelmets!' cried Biggles. 'We might as well have plaster ducks going up the wall, dear! We might as well have regency stripes!'

A terrible silence fell over the hut. The Group-Captain stared at Biggles for a very long time. Then his cat began to cough. Without another word, the Group-Captain snatched Bosie from the floor, and stomped out; echoingly.

The men cleared their throats, and shuffled, and murmured. After a few minutes, the door opened again, and the Group-Captain's aide-de-camp hurried in, with tiny, precise steps, and tossed back a golden forelock.

'He's very, *very* hurt,' he said. 'He's having one of his migraines. He says you're all to go off *right this minute* and bomb Hanover!'

The door slammed.

The men got up, slowly, and began to move out. Everyone ignored Biggles.

'It's suicide, putting a pelmet up in a room like that!' cried Biggles, but nobody listened.

'I *hate* Hanover,' muttered Algy to Ginger. 'It's such a *boring* route.'

'I could navigate a pretty way,' murmured Ginger, squeezing Algy's arm, as they walked towards their Wellington. 'We could go in low over Holland. The tulips'll be out. That'd be bona, wouldn't it, Biggles?'

'Go to hell!' snarled his Squadron-Leader, and pulled himself up into the plane. Algy rolled his eyes.

'Gawd help us all,' he muttered, 'she's come over masterful!'

He allowed Ginger to climb up through the belly hatch first, and helped him with an unhurried push. Biggles was already at the controls. The starboard engine fired, the port engine followed, the bomber swung out onto the runway, lumbered over the rutted concrete, and finally heaved itself into the cold East Anglian sky.

'Makes a change, having a closed cockpit,' shouted Algy from the co-pilot's seat, to break the frigid atmosphere, 'better for my rash.'

Biggles said nothing.

'Be like that,' said Algy. He pulled his mask over his mouth, and flicked the communications switch. 'Co-pilot to navigator,' he said, 'you wouldn't fancy that new Judy Garland tonight and a skate dinner on me, by any chance, dear?'

'Love it!' came back Ginger's eager crackle, on the open channel.

Squadron-Leader Bigglesworth, trained to a hair's breadth, did not react. He experienced eyes, emphasized with just the merest hint of mascara, stared straight ahead towards the Dutch coast, unmoistening. Only the sudden whitening of his knuckles on the controls betrayed the tensions of the inner man.

Which was why, betrayed by that rigid glower, he did not spot the Me 109 hurtling in on his starboard quarter until it was too late, and the bullets were pumping into wing and fuselage! Too late, he heard the anguished cry of Algy in his ears:

'Ooooh, they've hit a fuel lead, the port engine's packed up, there's oil pouring in all *over* me, we're losing height, what'll we do?'

'Hang on!' cried Biggles. 'Don't panic, I've had oil on my flying-suit a dozen times, you just soak it in a lukewarm solution of soap-flakes and engine solvent, but,' and here his voice rose above the stricken starboard motor, *'whatever you do, don't trying boiling it!'*

Algy gripped his knee.

'I didn't mean that about her skate dinner,' he shouted. Then he kicked open the bomb doors, and dropped. Ginger and the mid-upper gunner followed him. The tail-gunner was long gone.

Biggles waited until their parachutes flowered open, then he unbuckled his seatbelt, grabbed his douche-bag, and went out through the yawning bomb-bay.

It was not until the precise second when he pulled the rip-cord that he remembered about his parachute. But he was Biggles, so he merely grinned: some people would give their all for silk pyjamas, and some wouldn't. That was what life was all about.

He had just enough time to glance up through the shrouds and see the remnant tatters of his chute before he hit the Rotterdam ring-road, like a brick.

The Urban Diary of a Contemporary Gentleman

October

Thus called by the old Romans because in this month Fiats traditionally begin to rust in eight different places. Known by the Germans as *Edithholdenmonat*, since it is the time when the Common Publisher flocks to the shrine of the saint in Frankfurt in the hope of finding a miraculous cure, and by the British as *Christmas*, because it is when Carmen rollers and Cyprus sherry appear on television for the first time.

DAYS OF NOTE.

October 9.   St Dynorod.
October 12. St Bluecol.
October 18. St Valium.

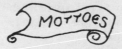

'A woman met on a topless French beach in August always looks more married outside a Bayswater hotel in October.'

'You take away more from a doctor's waiting-room in October than you ever bring into it.'

'Breakdown in October,
AA man in June.'

'A child's raincoat is always somewhere else.'

OCT. 1.

Wind from East last night. Out early, tile-gathering. Some fine sturdy varieties, esp. Old Lugless Garage, which falls with a clean, fast trajectory. Look for them

15

where you see their unmistakeable wedge-shape dents on boots, bonnets, children etc.

Today, I was privileged to watch a ginger cat fishing in our pond: Its technique is to scoop guppies (£2 each) into its mouth, and stare at me while it chews. When I greet it with the traditional brick, it makes a noise like breaking glass; this is because it has moved away suddenly from the greenhouse.

Ginger Cat With Guppie

OCT. 2.
Last of the pears fell off. We have had a good crop this year (8½), typical English Conference or perhaps Williams – not easy to tell, since by the time I get to them they are brown and flat and wet, not unlike small cowpats with wasps in.

Built a bonfire this afternoon. There is nothing like the smell of polystyrene smoke and the crackle of exploding deodorant canisters. A hysterical neighbour, fearful lest sparks ignite the cleaning fluid with which she is attempting to remove beer-stains from the avocado Dralon suite she has dragged onto her patio so that fluid fumes will not cause unsightly genetic disorders in her new foetus, persuades me to stamp the fire out. My soles melt. I now have a pair of gum uppers, to little point.

OCT. 3.
That fine, frost-snapping time of year when the fingers are so cold that the nut you have just removed from the

Volvo rear windscreen wiper in an attempt to discover why it stops in light showers drops from them and rolls down a drain. A good time, too, to pull the metallic strip from the anti-freeze canister so that the contents rot your shirt.

I have decided to get my bulbs in before it is too late. Last night, waking to the familiar noise of a late reveller losing his dinner on our Dutch wall, I switched on the bedside lamp, forgetting that I had put its bulb in the children's bathroom light, because I had taken the bulb from there to replace the one in the study Anglepoise broken when the thing suddenly keeled over and fell in my coffee. Groped into hall to remove hall lightbulb to put in bedside lamp, but bulb-glass broke away from little brass bit, filling hair with tiny shards; combed hair in dark, then afraid to move, since glass shards were now on carpet. Stood there for some time, listening to the wind whistling through the draught excluders.

This morning awoke to find other hands had been switching hall lights on and off; since upstairs and downstairs switches inter-relate, it was by now impossible to find out whether wires hanging from hall light fitting were on or off. Turned off mains, but could not remove little brass bit; pliers fell in eye.

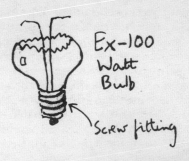

Walked to shops. Observed all the varieties of bulb on my walk, viz. 60-watt, 75-watt, 100-watt, 150-watt in bayonet fitting, spotlights, candle-bulbs in 25-watt and

40-watt bayonet *and* screw fittings, fairy lights, fluorescent tubing in 2-foot, 3-foot, 4-foot, 6-foot and 8-foot lengths, 8-watt night-light bulbs, 60-watt, 75-watt, 150-watt in screw fitting. Truly, richness in all things.

Needed 100-watt screw fitting bulbs, however.

But there is no call for them.

OCT. 4.

Awoke at 3 am, sweating heavily. Thought a croup was upon me, or even a grippe, necessitating some old and trusted remedy, such as 600,000 units of intra-muscular ampicillin, but found that winter moonlight was glinting off similarly glazed wife. Got up, found radiator red-hot; entire house throbbing like ship's boiler. Crawled downstairs, found time-switch reading 9 am, since not re-adjusted after mains switched back on.

Weather continues wet and blustery, especially in downstairs hall. Small son has got up in boiling heat, and opened all windows. Many interesting berries trodden into carpet.

OCT. 9.

Bright and crisp, after the damp spell. As if by magic, on a sunny corner of the front wall, ARSNEL POOFS has sprung up overnight.

Driving to work, I counted eighteen varieties of Madmen.

OCT. 11.

The apple-cheeked wife of a sturdy young Media Accounts Executive who hails from the other side of the A41 flyover today presented me with a fine brace of grouse which her husband had personally frozen. This, in our part of the world, is the traditional way of saying *Thank You* to someone who has allowed your children to smash his television set beyond repair. Some debate ensues in our kitchen as to the possible state of putrescence when frozen; my good lady is of the opinion that thawing will release enough bacilli to depopulate

18

The Common Grouse
[Lagopus Scoticus]

A.C.

most of Greater London. I scoff at her feminine temerity, and leave the plump little fellows in the boiler room.

By mid-afternoon, it smells like Scutari Hospital.

OCT. 13.

A rare difference of opinion with those good fellows, the dustmen. Normally, our relationship is warm, and based on mutual respect: I allow them to drop fish-heads and old bean cans on our lawn, and in return, they allow me to pick them up. On this occasion, however, they decline my invitation to remove the bin containing the grouse, on the grounds that they try to keep a nice clean truck. One of their number, a stocky fellow who seems to have only two fingers on his right hand, shouts over his departing shoulder that at least Doctor Crippen had the decency to bury *his* wife under the cellar-floor.

I decide to burn the offending bodies on the bonfire, and am intrigued to learn that my neighbour's solicitors are Twistleton, Ruggs, Furbelow and Schwarzbinder. Shropshire names, at a guess, with at least one ancestor following the grouter's trade.

OCT. 16.

A sharp white unexpected frost, reminding me that today would be a good time to lift the geraniums.

But not as good as yesterday.

Here is a useful tip: dead geraniums make an excellent

19

cover, when piled thickly, for old grouse bones, and will keep a ginger cat off them for nearly six minutes.

OCT. 18.
As the colder weather closes in, crowds of friendly denizens of the neighbouring acres come to be fed: this morning alone, trying to get through the kitchen to see why the aerial had slid off the chimney last night, filling the screen with twelve gently wobbling Rippons, I spotted a Lesser Daily, a pair of male Unigate Milkmen, a Bengal Grocer, and the shrilly screaming young of the late School Rota. They seem to subsist mainly on tea and chocolate wheaten biscuits, but are prepared to eat anything, from cold roast beef to wodka, and may often be found happily truffling around in a larder incautiously left unlocked.

It is not our way to treat them as pests, but if we do wish them to go away, the method is simplicity itself. I just ask them to help me lift something.

OCT. 21.
This morning, my son brought me some fresh-picked mushrooms, the palest beige pileus, delicate yellow lamellae, and a darkly attractive, almost chocolate stipe. Truly, there is no art but Nature's! Eagerly, I asked the boy where he had picked them.

Phoned Rentokil.

Egg of Unigate

20

Sprang up early, and took the car for a brisk push. Determined as I was to cut across country to the Brent Cross Shopping Centre, it was not long before I was queueing for an honest bus, fetching up – as I seem upon these occasions so often to do – against one of those dear old ladies who abound in these parts and who, given the merest prompting by the sympathetic naturalist, will divest themselves of the most fascinating lore. Within five minutes, she had explained in colourful detail about how the niggers were pushing the rates up, how an International Cabal of Jews were poisoning virgins by putting cocaine in the reservoirs, and how, when she had been taken sick after eating a dog suey at her local Chinese take-away, her Pakistani doctor had put his hands all over her and tried to get her drunk on Gee's linctus.

Brent Cross on market day is really something rather special! Since, in order to conserve the natural beauty of the countryside, parking space was made available for no more than thirty thousand cars, you may often see elderly men jumping on one another's Peugeots in the unceasing evolutionary drive for *parkingsraum*, St John's Ambulancemen rushing hither and yon with scarcely a second glance at the Millwall or Brentford supporters hanging from their colourful scarves, and the bright autumn air thick with Teflon pans and Moulimix parts as the cheery shoppers give vent to their irresistible passions.

Inside, you will find that craftsmen and traders have flocked from every point of the compass to sell their traditional wares. I never come away without buying something. Since I could not find the 100-watt screw-fitting bulb I sought, I chose instead a Formosan digital lacrosse game built into the head of a chiming fibre-tipped thermometer-knife.

It fell to bits on the way out, but when I took it back, the staff had changed and the shop itself was now a macrobiotic grocery.

Doctor No

DOCTORS are increasingly travelling incognito when on holiday because of fears that they will be called to help in a medical emergency.

Daily Telegraph

Beneath the brass sky, stepping gingerly from patch to scorching patch of gritty sand between the supine and motionless ranks of simmering mahogany flesh, the white English couple picked their serpentine way across the Riviera beach, the only moving things, like stricken relatives come to identify victims of some unimaginable act of arson.

A few yards from the shore at which the poisonous Mediterranean licked, they found a tiny space, hemmed by two other couples less blackened than the rest, but darkening, it seemed, with every passing second. The newcomer raised his sun-hat, wincing as the noonday pounced on his thinning scalp.

'Excusez-moi,' he said, haltingly, 'mais je – that is – wondered if this, er, space was ...?'

The couple on his left sat up.

'It's all right,' replied the man, 'we're English.'

'Not doctors, though,' said his wife quickly.

'Oh, no, definitely not doctors,' said her husband. 'English, but not doctors.'

'Not medical at all,' said his wife. 'I was never a nurse, even before I got married.'

'Nor was I,' said the woman on the other edge of the space, sitting up and re-fastening her top.

'I can vouch for that,' said her husband. 'Not being a doctor, I never ran into nurses. I remember thinking, down the pit, it's a good life being a miner, but it almost certainly means you won't marry anyone medical.' He squinted up at the white couple, shielding his eyes with his hand. 'You're not doctors, are you?'

'*Doctors?*' cried the newcomer, throwing back his head and laughing for some time, rocking back on his heels, slapping his ivory thigh. '*Us*, doctors? Ha-ha-ha, good God, my word, bloody hell, did you hear that, Alice?'

'Yes, Norman, how incredible, I thought, being taken for doctors when we're actually in the ...'

'Tyre business!'

' ... confectionery trade.'

They looked at one another. A gull flew by.

'We have a tyres and confectionery shop,' explained the man, after a time.

'How interesting,' said the woman on their left.

'Yes. They go very well together, actually,' said the white man, sitting down. His wife lowered herself beside him, removed her sun-dress, rooted for sun-oil in her beach-bag. A magazine, as she did so, fell out onto the sand.

The man beside her looked at it.

'Isn't that the *British Medical Journal*?' he said.

Everyone stared at it.

'*Is* it?' said the white woman. 'I wonder how it ...'

'Yes, it is!' cried her husband. 'We got it for the weight, you know. We like to take every possible precaution when travelling. We went to our newsagent, and we said, look, we're going to the South of France, it's a terrible time of year for flies, August, what do you suggest, and he said, you cannot beat the BMJ, I think he called it, it has weight, it has a shiny surface for easy wiping off of fly remnants, and you will not mind using it to swat flies with because there is no possible way in which you would want to read it, since there is nothing in it of any interest to non-medical people, it is utter gobbledegook from start to finish, it is a completely closed book as far as shoe and confectionery people are concerned.' He licked his lips. 'So we brought it.'

'I thought you said tyres and confectionery,' said the man on his left.

'I did, yes, I definitely did,' replied the white man, 'and that was, that was, that was because tyres and confectionery are our *main* trade, people come in for a bar of chocolate or a pound of those boiled things, sweets, and while they're in, we show them our wide range of tyres.'

'And vice-versa,' said his wife. 'But many of them coming in for a bar of Crunchie, for example, do not have cars, do they, Norman?'

'No.' He took off his hat again and wiped the sweat from his forehead with it. 'But ... but they all have feet. And we can often sell them a shoe or two. We find.' He glanced quickly at the man on his right. 'It must make a nice change for you, being on the surface?'

'What?'

'Rather than down the mine.'

'Oh. Ah. Yes, yes it is, yes you're right there, old man! Yes it's not like the Riviera at all, down the pit.'

'You have a remarkably slim build, for a miner,' said the white lady, 'if I may say so.'

'Yes, I do,' said the miner. He spent some time lighting a cigarette. When he at last removed it from his lips, he was smiling. 'That is because I do not in fact do any digging or shovelling or anything of that order. I look after the canaries.'

His wife turned to gaze out to sea, and began, very slowly, to oil her shins.

'I didn't know they still took canaries down mines,' said the white man. 'I thought they had instruments for assessing the atmosphere.'

The miner took a long draw on his cigarette.

'They do, yes, you're absolutely spot-on there, they do. They, we, take the canaries down for the singing. It is an old tradition. There is no other entertainment in the pit, as you probably know.'

'Ah,' said the white man, nodding. The miner lit another cigarette from his stub. His fingers were shaking slightly. The white man tutted. 'I say, old man, you shouldn't, I mean I hope I'm not out of order here, but

24

you really shouldn't smoke so much, as a miner, should
you?'

The man on his right said:

'Why? Can smoking be bad for you?'

The white man looked at him, for a time. The others
waited.

'Er,' muttered the white man, 'it's just that I seem to
have read somewhere about those experiments they
carried out with smoking mice.'

'He isn't smoking mice,' said the man on his right.

'No,' agreed the white man, nodding slowly, 'no, that
is true. You do have a point there. But don't miners run
the risk of some kind of chest complaint, anyway? Didn't
I see that on the the box, or in one of the confectionery
papers, perhaps? Isn't it called, er, sili . . .'

'IN THE EXTREME!' shouted his wife suddenly,
spilling vast gouts of Ambre Solaire. 'I remember now, it
was in *Toffee News*, they pointed out that it was silly in
the extreme to smoke down a coalmine, it could blow up,
it was much better to suck sweets!'

'Ah,' said the man on the right. Nobody said anything
else for a while. They took handfuls of sand from one side
of their legs, and put them down on the other side.
Sometimes they patted them flat. Then the man on the
right said:

'*We* have a canary, interestingly enough. But it doesn't
sing.'

'They don't always,' said the miner.

'Perhaps, when we're back home, you could come and
look at it,' said the man on the right. 'It may have
something wrong with it.'

'Ambrose doesn't do house calls,' said Ambrose's wife,
quickly.

'What?' said the canary's owner.

'You'd have to come during pit hours,' muttered
Ambrose. 'It really wouldn't be worth your while getting
filthy, they don't have to sing, they're quite decorative
just hopping about after a ball of wool, I find. Busy chap
like you.'

Everyone looked at the man on the right.

'Yes,' he said, 'yes, that's true, we are very busy, right now.'

'Doing what?' enquired the white man.

A ball bounced among them before the canary owner could answer, and was retrieved by two apologetic Swedes.

'I make goalposts,' said the man on the right, 'yes, that's what I do.'

'How remarkable!' exclaimed the white woman. 'One had never imagined goalposts being specially made, but of course, they have to be, don't they?'

'It's highly professional,' said the goalpost-maker, nodding. 'There's the angles, for one thing. It is illegal, under the rules of soccer, to have anything but a right-angled corner bit, as we call it. There's not many people know that. Furthermore . . .'

He broke off. A fearful shriek had cut through the heavy air.

The crowd sprang to its feet, peering into the aching glitter of the sea whence the noise had issued. Far off, a dark blob was making pitiful ripples on the silvered calm.

'Seems to be waving at someone,' murmured the miner.

'Probably enquiring about pedalo prices,' suggested the goalpost-maker.

The white man took a pair of binoculars from his beach-bag.

'Might be a baritone,' he said, 'rehearsing for . . . *Good God!*'

'What is it?' cried the other two.

'It's an Arab!' shouted the white man.

He was two lengths up when they hit the water, but the others had only paused to pull on flippers, and from then on, it was anybody's race.

Pope rules out sex in afterlife

The Pope has affirmed that Catholic teaching excludes sexual activity in the afterlife, although the risen would still be male or female. He said the resurrection meant not only bodily recovery but a new state of life.

Hallo. As you can doubtless imagine, ever since the above nugget appeared, shimmering, in last week's *Times*, the Vatican has been inundated with hysterical requests for clarification, and they have naturally turned to me, as an old friend, for assistance. What could I say but yes? It is, after all, Christmas, His Holiness has a lot on his plate in addition to its being a season of mutual caring, and I am only too glad to put my shoulder to the exegetical wheel and help in any way I can. As Auden so succinctly expressed it, we must love one another, or die.

Not, as it transpires, both.

Anyway, the Vatican has duly passed on to me several sackloads of enquiry, I have sorted the correspondence out into the major categories, and I shall endeavour to answer these queries as fully and as helpfully as I can. I have also, since some categories lead naturally into others, attempted to give this little catechism a sequence.

Thank you.

What is all this about bodily recovery? I thought we got wings and a quoit. I know a number of cartoonists, and they say everybody stands about on clouds, except when they have to come back as poltergeists.

You are mixing two things up. It is a common mistake. Upon death, it is true, you float up to Heaven. You do not have a body *as such*, it is more a sort of outline, to facilitate cartooning: you leave your body behind in a box, and upon arrival at what we call Heaven's Gate, you get a cloakroom ticket. This enables you to claim your body when the Resurrection comes, which is what you have been mixing up with Heaven. At the Resurrection, you get your body back and carry on as normal. Nearly normal.

This body I get back: what sort of shape will it be in?
It will have been what we call *glorified*, i.e. restored. It will be in perfect nick, no rubbish. It may be that if you have snuffed it while bald, or during an earthquake or similar, you will not at first recognize it. That is why it is *absolutely essential* to hang on to your ticket.

Suppose there is an administrative cock-up? I recently deposited my briefcase at Euston Left Luggage Office, and when I returned the next day with my ticket, they gave me an umbrella, due to both halves of said ticket matching. I do not wish to be resurrected with a bamboo handle where my head is supposed to be, do I?
There is no question of this happening. I have discussed your query with His Holiness, who tells me the Almighty expects to have the whole thing on the computer by then.

Thank you very much. If my recent experience in trying to get a bloody driving licence out of Swansea is anything to go by, I shall probably come back as a gas bill. If I do not, and all the tickets match up etcetera, will my body have any clothes on? Obviously, I intend getting buried in my blue three-piece with the chalk-stripe, but as it is already beginning to rot under the arms, what happens if it all falls to bits before the Resurrection?
Many people have asked that, and the Vatican has been able to reassure all enquiries, categorically, that suiting will also be glorified to avoid possible embarrassment. This means that not only will your blue chalk-stripe be pristine under the arms, there will be no stains on your tie, either.

Having been fully restored but not allowed sex, is this

*not going to be a bit unsettling? I have heard what goes
on in the Navy, etc.*

No one said anything about *fully* restored. If, for
example, you were restoring a Sheraton sideboard, you
would not choose to put the original woodworm back,
would you? That is the way we feel about sex, up the
Vatican. You will be restored, but without a couple of
glands that should never have been there in the first
place.

*What is the point, then, of being resurrected as male and
female?*

You have to get your original body back. These will have
beards, busts, etc. One lot will obviously be different
from the other lot. You will look exactly as you looked in
your prime.

Can I be a bit taller?

No.

*What about a peculiar walk? I have seen a lot of doctors,
but they say there is nothing they can do, I shall have to
live with it. I should not like to think I was in for an
eternity of people pointing in the street.*

That depends entirely upon whether you had the
peculiar walk before or after your prime. If the former,
there is not a lot He can do, despite His infinite wisdom.
Console yourself with the thought that it might not look
so peculiar to people after a few billion years. Those
people who have a peculiar walk as the result of sex, of
course, will find that it clears up after resurrection.

*I'm sorry to come back to sex, it is not that I am obsessed
or anything, but would the none-at-all rule also apply to
Saturdays?*

I see I have not made His Holiness clear. Once these
glands are out, they are out. You cannot just pop them in
for the weekend.

*Does this glorification apply to domestic premises?
When I am resurrected and walk the earth again, will I
find they have put the loft back at 14 Palmerston
Crescent, Hendon? We spent a fortune having it
converted into a pine-panelled den, never mind all the*

upheaval and dust everywhere. Am I to assume it will be restored in my absence, plus all the tea-chests back with old hats in?

No, you are on safe ground there. Houses do not have immortal souls, they do not float up and get wings and then get resurrected, they stay where they are. If the Almighty *was* going to restore them not only would they almost certainly revert to primordial slime, which would be of no use to anyone, the paperwork would be totally unmanageable. Even for Him. Planning permission alone could take eons.

All right, but who would be living there? If the previous occupier popped his clogs in situ, and then the same thing happened to us twenty years later, who gets the house? I certainly would not consider sharing it with the old buggers we inherited it from. I do not wish to speak ill of the dead, but they left it filthy.

I have raised this matter with His Holiness, who says that, in certain special circumstances, some houses may have to be glorified into flats. Of course, this will reduce the accommodation, but bear in mind that since the glands we mentioned will not be resurrected, you will not need bedrooms for the children. Also, it should be remembered that because there is no sex, many couples may now be prepared not to have separate bedrooms. This may be something you wish to discuss with your wife before dying.

I suppose, then, that there is no hope of coming back and finding the car glorified?

Correct. I am afraid that you will have to accept the possibility of being resurrected and finding nothing but a pile of brown dust. If it has been undersealed, of course, you might find a wing. It rather depends how long you have to be in Heaven before the Day of Resurrection comes. It could take us all by surprise, and you could find yourself back again with nothing worse than a flat battery.

The Republic: Book XI

Efforts by Oxford University to appoint a Greek as a lecturer in Classical Philosophy have been met by an invitation from the Department of Employment to take the vacancy to the local Job Centre and advertise it to Britain's unemployed. – The Guardian.

I went down the Job Centre yesterday morning, didn't I, with Glaucon, the son of Ariston, on account of the course being waterlogged at Haydock and Plumpton and the bleeding betting-shop shut also the pubs not open yet, so where else can you go when it's bucketing down? And don't say 'back home' if you haven't seen my old woman with her teeth out, she never puts 'em in until after *Crown Court*, due to ulcers.

'I hate this place, Glaucon,' I said, 'it smells of vacancies. In an ideal state, they'd do away with employment.'

'The main thing, Socrates,' said Glaucon, 'is not to catch their eye. If you catch their eye, it's Next Please, and before you know it, you're up Woollies packing department.'

'You do not have to tell me, son,' I said. 'I had one of them long brown coats on once, you feel like muck. Do this, do that. June 18, 1956. Also, they stand by the staff exit when you clock off and they steal stuff what has inadvertently fallen into your pockets. If this is work, I told 'em, you can bloody keep it, thank you very much.'

'In an ideal state,' said Glaucon, 'we would not have to work, would we, Socrates?'

'Bloody right,' I explained. 'I did not spend six years of World War Two hiding in my auntie's loft to keep the world safe for democracy in order to come out and have

31

my pockets inspected for bottles of HP.'

'You were a conscientious objector then, Socrates?'

'Naturally. It was what we call a classic clash between an unjust authority and a just individual. They refused to recognize my objection.'

'What did you object to?'

'I objected to being shot at, Glaucon. I did not muck about claiming I was a Quaker or nothing, that would have been dishonest, and anyway they would have conscripted you as a porridge supervisor or something. I just come right out and give 'em the full force of rational argument before buggering off while their backs were turned and nipping up the loft. In the event, I was proved right. Germany was defeated, and I come down again.'

'A victory for reason, Socrates,' said Glaucon.

'Definitely.' I looked at my watch. 'In an ideal state, Glaucon, they would have opened the bloody pubs by now. Also invented sunnink to remove water during the flat season. Have you ever noticed that we can put men on the Moon but are unable to do sod all about soft going at Kempton?'

'Morning all!'

We looked up. It was Cephalus, father of Pole-marchus. He is not half spry for his age, and puts it all down to not having worked since observing how far marching down from bloody Jarrow got anybody, also to smoking other people's Woodbines.

'What are you doing here, Cephalus?' enquired Glaucon, a logical question given that the old man has been known to leave a free pint untouched at the very mention of the word job.

'I come here to gloat,' replied Cephalus, 'on account of I was 65 last Monday and they cannot lay a finger on me no more. I come in regular to drop my fag-ends in their khazi, also put all the forms back in the stands upside down. In an ideal state, Glaucon, it is up to the just man to keep the bastards on the hop, am I right, Socrates?'

'Definitely,' I said.

'Also, I like looking at that new blackie on Supplementary Benefits A-G with the big knockers.'

We stared at her for a time.

'In an ideal state,' propounded Glaucon, wiping his lip on his cap, 'we could get that on the NHS. Which reminds me, Socrates, is it better to be beautiful than good?'

I pondered the point for a time.

'It is all right being beautiful, and it is all right being good,' I said, 'but the best thing is to have a car.'

'I would dispute that, Socrates,' said Thrasymachus of Chalcedon, who had just come in to see if there were any vacancies for astronauts on account of he had promised his wife to settle on a career, now that the children were grown up and not bringing in any family allowance. 'In my opinion, it is better to have a bicycle.'

'Because it is healthier, also you can nip in and out, Thrasymachus of Chalcedon?' enquired Glaucon.

'No, Glaucon,' replied Thrasymachus. 'Because if you have a car they only come round and ask you where you nicked it.'

'In an ideal state,' advanced Cephalus, 'they'd give you them little red Fiats on the NHS, wouldn't they, Socrates?'

'That is what philosophy calls a dodgy one, Cephalus,' I informed him. 'That is similar to the one concerning which way the water goes down the plughole south of the Equator to which we addressed ourselves up the Rat and Cockle at our last session. According to Plato, in an ideal state there wouldn't be any Wops at all, sending their cheap rubbish over here and putting people out of work. Before you know it, there will be three million amateur unemployed filling up job centres. You and me won't even be able to come in out of the rain, never mind getting a decent seat near the window.'

The disciples considered this for a time.

'I thought Plato was a dog,' announced Thrasymachus of Chalcedon at last. 'I seen him up Saturday morning pictures. He hangs about with a duck.'

'Mouse, you mean,' said Glaucon.

'Plato a *dog*?' I cried, losing for a moment my philosophical calm. 'Do you know nothing? Apart from formulating the complex system known as *Backing Second Favourites For A Place*, which admittedly still requires some fine logical tuning due to where him and me was six hundred quid down last season, Plato is the man primarily responsible for leading the philosophical search for the perfect job. What he calls the Essential Employment, the one from which all other employments derive as flawed imitations.'

They were silent. I sensed an unease among them.

'Perfect job, Socrates?' enquired Glaucon. 'After all our long discussions, are you telling us you are knocking around with someone seeking to undermine our entire ethical bleeding framework?'

I smiled tolerantly.

'In an ideal state, Glaucon,' I replied, 'they'd have twerps like you made into bookends.' I looked slowly from one to another. 'The ideal job, as laid down by Plato in his seminal work which is not yet written out but if it ever is will probably be entitled *A Major Conversation with Socrates in the Back of the Bus Coming Home from the Bloody Cesarewitch*, the ideal job is one for which you are paid large sums for doing absolutely nothing at all. It is, leave us face it, pupils, the only rational extension if we start from the premise that the worst possible job is one where you get paid nothing for working your bloody wossnames off, am I right?'

They nodded.

'But tell us, Socrates,' said Glaucon, 'what form would this ideal job take if we ever run across the bugger?'

'Form,' I answered, 'is not a term Plato would fancy. The *essence* of this job, however, would be where you had nice warm comfortable premises, all rent and expenses paid, hot dinners twice a day plus cooked breakfast and them little triangular Spam sandwiches at tea-time, free access to the company's booze cupboard twenty-four hours a day, and servants to run around after you, making beds and cups of tea etcetera etcetera. You would not have to move out of said premises to go to work, on account of the work would consist of people coming in and sitting around nattering with you all day and everybody getting plastered on free brown sherry.'

'Or whisky, Socrates?'

'Or whisky, Thrasymachus of Chalcedon.'

'Stone me!' murmured Cephalus. 'That is what I *call* an ideal job.'

He sighed. We all did. After a bit, I got up.

'There is no point sitting around here, pupils, dreaming impossible bloody dreams,' I said. 'Especially as they are now open.'

We walked to the door, and I was just going through it when one of the clerks called out:

'Oy, any of you layabouts fancy a lectureship in Classical Phil –'

We was out of there like bullets, I don't mind saying!

'Nearly caught us that time,' said Glaucon.

I eyed the summoned butler with that immemorial Look which down the arches of the years had blanched the swarthy Saracen and chilled through thermal mail to freeze the presumptuous Norman where he stood.

'Bring me,' I thundered, 'my best nib and a bottle of Unigate vitriol, that I may counter this iniquity and leave th'escutcheon pure!'

I do not often say *th'*; despite the obligations of *noblesse*, the strain was showing. I think, however, the nuances were lost upon the butler: she had but recently joined us from one of Austria's educationally sub-normal hamlets, and the only English words she knew were barry and manilow. Fearing, from my tone and Look, some imminent reprimand, she turned and scuttled off to fuse the Hoover and defrost the stove.

'Wossup, pater?' enquired my heir, removing his head from the polythene bag and stoppering his Bostik. 'Is it one of your turns?'

'It is this!' I roared, with such force that tacks sprang from the walls and the elegant oakette panelling of the baronial dining alcove peeled suddenly from its sturdy battens. I waved the just-delivered *Radio Times* beneath his sticky nose. The fresh ochre cheeks of boyhood paled. Tears pricked at my eyes as I watched his lips move painfully through the ensnaring syllables.

'Stone me, pater!' he exclaimed, at last. 'They are doing the Six Great Families of Brian –'

'Britain.'

'– of Britain, and we are not there! Who are these Russells and Percys and Howards, anyway?'

I ran my hand through the lad's hair. I looked at my fingers.

'This purple comes off,' I said.

'Sorry, pater,' said the brave little fellow. 'I will go back to the shop and aerosol the bugger's Metro.'

I slapped his back, setting his dangling safety-pins a-jingle.

'That's the spirit, son!' I cried. 'That is the code of the Corens! *Nemo me impune lacessit*, eh?'

'They a group?' he said.

I looked at him.

'Try to remember, lad,' I said, 'that you are the scion of an ancient line no whit less noble than the Howards of whom we are about to hear so much, doubtless because *their* scion is the Chairman of the BBC.'

'Hang about, pater,' cried the boy, 'isn't he the same bloke who give his house so's they could film *Birkenhead Revisited* with all them bums?'

I nodded.

'*That* was ITV,' said my son. 'He puts it about a bit, don't he?'

'That is the way it is with the older families,' I replied. 'There was a time when your paternal great-grandfather himself had not one but two wet-fish shops.'

'Bloody hell!' he exclaimed. 'All that skate!'

'Quite,' I said. I drew my comfy old Habitat beanbag a little closer to the roaring radiator, and banged at the airlock with my crusty reject briar. 'Perhaps it is time that you learned a little of your ancestry, since the BBC has patently chosen to ignore it. Does the name Coren the Wake mean anything to you?'

His narrow brows knitted pitifully.

'I think we done him up history,' he said, 'din't he live in a bog and rough up the Nomads?'

'Normans,' I murmured. 'Yes, that's more or less correct, although he didn't fight personally. His job was to go around with a long pole and bang on the windows, so that the soldiers would get up in time. It was an extremely important position. Always remember, laddie, it is not necessarily the most glamorous men who make the most history.'

The boy nodded sagely.

'You can look like a pig, these days,' he said. 'Take Mick Jagger.'

'Or take,' I said, quickly, 'Robin Coren and his Merry Men.'

'I know about *them*! They were an enormous bloody band, weren't they, pater?'

'Absolutely correct! And that was hundreds of years before big bands became fashionable. They would quote for functions anywhere in the realm. Their motto was: *No Job Too Large Or Small*. They needed several carts. Your ancestor himself doubled on dulcimer and drums.'

'Fantastic!'

'*And* they did novelty numbers.' I refilled my pipe, slowly. 'Have you heard of the Black Prince?'

'He was never a Coren, too?' gasped the boy.

'Robin's brother,' I said. 'He used to sing *Sonny Boy*, *April Showers*, *Shine on Harvest Moon*, *Makin' Whoopee*. His yellow gloves are in the British Museum, somewhere.' I lit up, and let the blue clouds thin. 'Subsequently, though, there was something of a decline. The Middle Ages were a fallow, not to say bleak, period in our fortunes: Thomas à Coren was killed in Canterbury Cathedral, thanks to the tragic combination of a wormy ladder and a heavy bucket, Coren of Arc heard voices from God but they threw him in the bin before he could get any publicity, and Wat Coren was a total failure from the outset.'

'Was Wat Coren one of them peasant leaders, pater?'

'No, son, Wat Coren was a consumer magazine aimed at a general public wishing to distinguish between members of the family, but nobody wanted to. It was the brain-child of Geoffrey Coren, your illustrious literary ancestor, who went by coach to Canterbury once, but they wouldn't let him inside because of the herring, so he sat on the roof on his own and made up stories to amuse himself. He would have been even more illustrious if they had amused anyone else. The final blow for our family came just at the end of the Middle Ages, when King Henry VII hanged Perkin Coren.'

'What had he done?'

'Nothing. They needed someone to test the gallows.'

'Bloody hell, pater, that was a big strong, wasn't it?'

'They gave him a groat for doing it, but it fell out of his fingers when he dropped and it rolled down a drain. I am afraid one must face the sad fact that Perkin was a bit simple.'

'Did things improve after the Middle Ages, pater?' enquired the lad.

I struck another vesta, and blew a matchless ring.

'Not immediately,' I said. 'Under Henry VIII, gluttony, alcoholism, and adultery flourished as never before, and led, unfortunately, to the notorious Dissolution of the Corens. However, things improved with

Elizabeth. Your intrepid forebear, Walter Coren, was one of the first men to bring back tobacco from the American colonies.'

'Cor! Did she knight him?'

'No, she threw him in the Tower. He was only allowed two hundred, and the Customs found twelve hundred down his galligaskins, plus four bottles of potato cointreau. But it was there in the Tower he had the time to sit down and write.'

'I seen that on the telly!' cried my heir excitedly. 'Where Paul Robeson is Queen Elizabeth. Was that the book what was to become *A History of the World*, pater?'

'Unfortunately not,' I replied. 'Walter had an appalling memory. It was the book which was to become *A History of the World Since Last Tuesday*. Not surprisingly, perhaps, it was never published. However, his revolutionary theory challenging the belief that the earth was flat received much attention, if only because the fashionable idea was that it might be round. Oblong was something new.'

'Was Walter the most famous Coren scientist, pater?'

'Until Isaac Coren came along. That was some fifty years later, of course, and roughly thirty years after the wicked Guy Coren changed the whole face of contemporary begging. Isaac Coren was sitting under a tree one day, when an apple fell on him. He immediately saw that some irresistible force drew fruit to earth; he snatched up a pencil and paper, scribbled a few quick calculations on a scrap of paper, and opened a greengrocer's. He, too, became a legend: from those humble beginnings, he was soon broke.'

'How come, pater?'

'The tree he built the shop under died. Isaac spent a whole year waiting for stock to fall onto his shelves, and nothing happened. You can read it in Samuel Coren's Diary.'

'About the greengrocer's shop?' enquired my son.

'No,' I replied. 'What you can read is *Nothing happened*. It is there on every page. I am afraid old Sam rather missed the boat when it came to the diary market. Had he lived a century later, life as a Coren would have been immeasurably more eventful. I am speaking, of course, of the days of Bonnie Charlie Coren, the Middle-Aged Pretender, who marched down from Scotland in 1730 at the head of three men, strode unannounced into the House of Commons, and asked if they wanted the windows done.' I glanced from my heir's rapt yawn to the *Radio Times*, and curled the family lip. 'I doubt, my boy, whether there is a Fitzgerald or a Percy who could lay claim to that! Nor, as I recall, was there ever a Beau Howard.'

The lad's eyes snapped open, on a sudden.

'Was there a Bo Coren, pater?'

'Indeed there was.'

'Did she have big things, pater?'

I stared at him. It is something I have often to do, I find.

'Beau Coren,' I replied, 'was a man. His clothes were famous all over Regency London.'

'Oh,' said the boy. 'What was so special about them, pater?'

'What was so special about them, lad,' I replied, 'was that if you hired the whole suit, he threw in the shirt absolutely free! Is there a Russell or a Hamilton of whom *that* was ever said?'

The boy stood up, and sleeved an errant nostril.

'I shun't think so, pater,' he said. He rooted in his iridescent locks. 'Being famous is all a matter of being in the right place at the right time, innit?'

I nodded, and tapped my cold pipe out.

'Yes, Elvis,' I said.

From The Diary of Samuel Pepys Jnr.

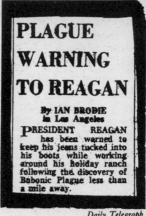

PLAGUE WARNING TO REAGAN

By IAN BRODIE
in Los Angeles

PRESIDENT REAGAN has been warned to keep his jeans tucked into his boots while working around his holiday ranch following the discovery of Bubonic Plague less than a mile away.

Daily Telegraph

AUGUST

20. Up betimes, and some unsettlynge grutchings of pain in the Great Bowel, I praye God not the Sicknesse but meerly a Winde arising from my having fasted for so long. I truste that this new Executone Bjorn Borg Grape 'n' Clam Diet is not too austere at onlie three hundred calories *per diem*, already I find myselfe unable to jogge as heretofore, being too weery to zippe up my trackesuite.

Downstayres, to where my dear children are at breakfaste in our elegant nooke and my son Samuel III much agitated at my pallor, admonishing mee earnestly not to drive to my office. His concerne touches mee deeplie, but it is shortlie out that he fears that, should I indeed have contrackted the Sicknesse, I wil contaminate the Mercedes which he has bespoke this nighte for a heavy date and does not wish for himselfe or his beloved that they catch buboes from the upholesterie. My younger daughter enraged at this; she and I were ever moste close, and teers sprynge to her fair eyes at the thoughte of my Deth, since she fears that I do not carrye enough insurance to see her through college.

Yet further dischorde thereat attends, however, my

elder daughter declayming the opinion that shee has the prioritie distrainte, since while it is possible to work one's way through college, it is not possible to work one's way through analysis, it is presentlye runninge out at around five hundred per session and there are many yeers ahead, they have not yet even reached the poynte at which she muste recognyze her pathological hatred of her father and rejecte himme.

I turne thereat to my deer wyfe who is wobblynge upon the elecrical exerciser, to supplicate her tenderest intervention in these matters touchynge upon our familie; but shee lets out such a shriek at my elder daughter for darynge to place her sanity above her mother's need for a new buste and bobbed nose, five thousand minimum, thatte I creepe from the house in despayre.

21. Up early, and downe to meet with Doctor Schumacher at his office, my Guttes being no better though no Lumpes, thanke God, appearyng; some Ague of the joyntes, but doubtless due to my deer wyfe takynge the circumspect precaution of lettynge me sleepe in the yarde.

I am met by Doctor Schumacher's nurseperson, a goodlie buxome soul who takes my hat and coate wyth rubber gloves and throwes them in the trash, and bids me enter the surgerie. Within minutes, the Doctor appeares upon the closed circuit screene above my head, explayninge that there is much Sicknesse about in the City and hee is therefore takynge his surgerie from his jacuzzi in Palm Springs, and solicitously enquires of mee what might be the trouble?

I descrybe my distressing symptoms to him, and he listens most carefully, noddynge from tyme to tyme. When I have finished, I ask him what he thinkes it might be, and he replyes that he thinkes it might be, anything from five hundred to a thousand, dependynge upon whether I require a second visit. I tell him that I praye it is not the Plague, and hee is very sympathetic, reminding mee that if it is Plague it would mean puttynge the house on the market and talkynge to his brother Sam atte the Schumacher Finance & Loan. Hee would, since I was an olde and deere friend as well as a patient, put in a good word with his brother, but his advyce to mee was that if I was pulling downe less than a hundred thousand a yeare, I would be extreamely unwise even to thinke about contrackting the Plague. If I did catche it, *nolens volens,* his professional opinion was that I shoulde cutte my losses, and die.

To my office later, and much excitement! No lesse than three Executive Vice-Presidents have swoll'd up in the nighte and there is much eeger jockeyinge for their positions. This hath thrown us all into a great whirl, and if th'Almighty spares mee yet strikes down Kowalksi and Rappaport, I could yette emerge from the Sicknesse as Senior Head of Sales Conceptualization (South).

Home at my most fleete to impart the news to my deere wyfe, but she away at her yoghurt class, and the lockes all changed. I can see my deere children, through the windowes, but they shreeke at me to take myselfe to a goodlie distance.

22. Up at dawne shakynge with a Palsie and dredfull red weals upon my backe; but these, I thinke, due not to the Sicknesse but to my sleepynge on the rail-roade trackes. Rose betimes, and hobbled to the barber, my razor being at home; a fyne discourse with the learned man, hee being of the opinion that the Plague is due to the blackamoors and will be cured only upon the application of shotgunnes; since I grow exceedynge uneasy at talke of the Sicknesse, I turn the topicke to the Recession, and fynde the man eeger of economicke solution: since the Recession can onlie be due to the blackamoors, shotgunnes are the one sure answer. Wee are keenlie discussing the twinne matters of Communism and Homosexualitie, the honeste barber holding that these are being spread daily through the realm by the blackamoors, when there is a great tumulte above our

44

heads from the television screen, announcynge thatte a fortunate houseperson from the fayre city of Boise, Idaho, has just won ten thousand dollars on *Guess My Bubo!*, the newest game showe, upon which contestants suff'ring all manner of noxious infections – quinsy, thrush, stone, head-mould, pox, dropsie, convulsions, wormes, imposthume, scurvy – pass before a jurie of their peeres, who have to discover the *genuine* sufferer of the Plague: should hee deceive them all, hee receives not onlie ten thousand dollars, but also cosmetick em-balmynge to resemble the movie star of his or her choyce, a genuine mahoganette coffin with near-brass handels, and free cleaning of his premises, after his interment, by a top-name fumigator!

Truly, God Almighty smiles upon this His countrie!

From the barber, much cheered in spirit, but founde increasing traffic in the streetes of drear processions of mourners as the Sicknesse takes holde; this so distressed me, I turned into a hostelry, despyte the rigors of my diet, in search of a revyvinge cordial, styrred not shaken. The concoction not entirely to my lykinge, I enquired of its maker as to the whereaboutes of the regular barman; and was forwyth informed that he had juste that morning made a killynge upon the Stock Market and retired to the Bahamas.

Apparently, upon the very fyrste winde of the Plague, he had gone heavily into Funeral Parlour stock.

25. Up betimes, the 6.40 Rock Island freight having made an unconscionable noise a-shuntynge, and telephoned my deere wyfe; an unknowne man answeringe, I was greatly puzzled, the hour being so early, whereat my deere wyfe came upon the line to informe me that my elder daughter havynge persuaded her, after deep and meaningfull discussions with her analyst, that the collapse of Western Civilization was entyrely due to the destructive infibulations of the one-to-one relation-shyppe, she had therefore seized upon the fortuitous opportunitie presented by the Plague to replace me with

45

Clyde, a major garbage operative. I immediately replyed that I had it on the very best authoritie that the collapse of Western Civilization was, in facte, entyrely due to blackamoors; at which my deere wyfe enquired whether I should care to come round and saye that to Clyde's face.

Not wishing to avayle myselfe of this dubious offer, I repaired instead, through the increasingly emptie streetes, to what is now my regular hostelrie; I fynde that by dropping a grape into my dry martini, I am enabled both to satisfy my dietry strictures and simultaneously to alleviate my wretchednesse. Though it was yet but seven o'clock, the place was full of unshaven men in three-piece suits: upon enquirie, I ascertained that these were lawyers who had spent the whole of the previous night celebrating a major landmarke, nay, a very watershedde, in the historie of human litigation!

It transpyred that the next-of-kin of a woman dead of the Plague in Redwing, Minnesota, had successfully sued the owner of the barn in which expert evidence had established that the offendynge rat had been born and bred, for one hundred million dollars, the attorney being in for thirtie per cent of the grosse. With upwardes of six thousand soules now perishing daily in California alone, is it any wonder that the lawyers were dancing upon the tables?

26. To my office early, all now assured that I am sufferynge but a Colicke, but no great joye to be gleaned: Kowalski and Rappaport in seeming great healthe, and, yet more grave, my own sales area grievously dwindled through the Sicknesse. Commissions may be well downe this quarter.

However, much brightened by a Presidential broadcast at noon, our beloved Leader appearing hale and lumplesse, his trousers tucked into his bootes after a fashion now recognized as one of the greatest decisions of his career. His horse also in evident high spirits. Briefly, his message is that, with some thirty millions now neatly dead, the unemployment dilemma has vanished at a stroke; further, given the unhealthy proximity in which the inhabitants had chosen to live, the ghetto problem was now a thynge of the paste. At longe laste. The Shinynge City was in view! Certainly, I cannot have been alone in noting yet another new twinkle in his already sparkling eye, and it may well be that the Rumours concerning the *fons et origo* of the Sicknesse may not be as unfounded as I first conceived them to be. No doubt, in the fulnesse of tyme, credit will emerge where it is due; certain it is, the Plague hath been good for Businesse, and I should not bee the fyrste to remark that the businesse of America is Businesse!

Of course, the matter must not be allowed to get out of hande; as our great Leader took paynes to enunciate, enough was enough, and a method should now be soughte of eradicating the Plague swiftlie, much as had been achieved during its successful visitation of my namesake's London, with a purgative conflagration. Sufferers should be quietly removed to prevent further spreading of the Sicknesse. To that ende, he had discharged his trustie colleague, Mr Caspar Weinberger, with the dutie of discovering some device which could be counted upon to destroye people, while leaving property intact.

Ourselves to Know

Sunday Times

Mr Henry Fickling threw open the kitchen door, flared his nostrils, expanded his chest, rubbed his hands together, beamed an iridescent beam.

'Bacon!' he cried. 'There is nothing like the smell of old *piggus piggus* crackling in the pan!'

From the kitchen table, not glancing up from his cornflakes, his son muttered:

'Old what?'

'Dear God, Doreen!' exclaimed Fickling. 'Stap me vittles! Sacré coeur! The ignorance of boys today! I blame the change in diet, do I not?'

'Yes, dear,' said his wife, cracking an egg.

'When I was a lad, we never went out without a big spoon of Scott's Emotion inside us. It was made from fish. Consequently, it enlarged the brain like nobody's business.'

His daughter put down the *TV Times* and stared at him.

'Why on earth was it called Scott's Emotion?' she said.

Henry Fickling sighed.

'How short a thing is mortal memory,' he murmured, 'as Freddie Mills so succinctly put it. For your information, Tracy, it was Scott's Emotion on account of he brought it back with him from the North Pole. It had this picture on the bottle, showing him with a shark on his back. The stuff was made out of its liver.'

'There aren't any sharks at the North Pole,' said his son, through a piece of toast.

'Don't contradict your father,' said Doreen Fickling.

'Anyway,' said the boy, 'it was the South Pole Scott

went to, and there aren't any sharks there, either.' He looked at his father. 'You're probably thinking of penguins.'

'*Penguins?*' shrieked Henry Fickling. He slapped his thigh. He roared aloud. He snatched a handful of kitchen roll and dabbed his streaming eyes. 'Did you hear that, Mother? Answer me this, clever dick, if what you're implicating is true, how is it that the label did not show Colonel Scott with a penguin on his back? Are you suggesting that I grew up, moreover, on penguin liver oil, which is what Scott's Emotion was comprised with?'

The boy shrugged.

'Something's wrong somewhere,' he said. 'Because, in the first place, Scott never came back from the Pole.'

His father leaned over the table, and poked his son in the chest with a trembling forefinger.

'Never came back?' he shouted. '*Never came back?* Then how did the shark get here, may I ask? Did it bloody walk?'

'I don't know,' said the boy, 'it's your shark. Maybe it was Amundsen.'

'A mundsen? What is this boy talking about, Mother? Penguins, mundsens, he must be a laughing-stock up the comprehensive, am I right? As I understand it, Nigel, your entire view of the matter is based on the hypotenuse that instead of coming home and going into commercial medicine and duck-painting, Colonel Scott chose instead to stay at the North Pole walking around with a mundsen on his back. Does that seem logical to you, Doreen?'

'Here's your breakfast, dear,' said his wife.

Henry Fickling banged his plate on the table, and sat down in front of it.

'Respect for learning,' he snapped, 'where has it gone? Too busy sticking razor blades up their nostrils and watching Elton Lulu.'

His son licked the last cornflake from his spoon, and stared at Henry Fickling for some time. Finally, he said:

'It's not *piggus piggus*.'

His father froze, a forked rasher wobbling before his motionless lip. After a few moments, he put the fork down.

'What isn't?' he said, through his teeth.

'Pig,' said the boy. 'The Latin for pig is *porcus.*'

Mrs Fickling put down her spatula, as the familiar vein in her husband's temple began to throb like a lugworm.

'I remember!' she cried. 'It was Scott's *Emulsion!*'

Fickling, like a diverted rhino, swung round in his chair.

'Oh really? Doubtless, we were supposed to slap it on the bloody ceiling? Came home from the Pole with the secret of washable skirtings, did he? Set himself up as COLONEL SCOTT PAINTER & DECORATOR NO JOB TOO LARGE OR SMALL LET US QUOTE YOU? Well, well, well, who says you don't learn something new every day? When I came in here this morning, just a few short minutes ago, I was totally ignorant of the fact that England's greatest hero made his name out of refurbishing domestic premises with quarts of tasteful eau-de-nil penguin derivative!' He swivelled back towards his breakfast, but his wife's diversionary tactic came to naught. He fixed his son with a terrible eye. '*Porcus,*' he snapped, 'is Latin for *roast* pig, am I right, Doreen?'

'Or shoulder,' said his wife.

'Or shoulder,' said Fickling. His eyes did not move from his son's. Eventually, the boy took another piece of toast, and buttered it slowly.

'And –' he unscrewed the marmalade jar carefully, '– bacon?'

'I'm very glad you asked me that,' replied his father. 'Bacon is not from the Latin *baconus,* which is something else entirely and a bit advanced for me to go into with a non-classicalist, but takes its name from Sir Francis Bacon, as the famous anecdote relates. One night, Sir Francis was up his club playing brag with the Duke of Sandwich and William Shakespeare and similar, arguing about who was going to write *Charley's Aunt*, I believe it was, when the Earl of Sandwich suddenly said: "Hang about, anyone fancy a bite to eat?" Well, they called the chef over, and he said he c ouldn't do a proper hot dinner, all he had was a bit of pig in the fridge but no sprouts or stuffing or anything of that nature; so Bacon said: "Look, if you fry up the meat and stick it between a couple of slices of Wonderloaf, that'll keep us going for a bit." And that's how bacon was invented.'

'Magic,' murmured his son, trying not to look at his sister.

'There wasn't much wrong with Bacon's brains,' nodded Fickling. "Course, that was before the apple fell on his head.'

His son slid sideways to the floor, and lay there for a time, gasping. Quickly, his mother scuttled across, helped him up, and, shoving his sister, too, before her, pushed them out of the kitchen.

'What was all that about?' enquired Fickling, cleaning his plate with a crust.

'Nothing.' She smoothed her apron, cleared her throat, poked a wisp of hair back, put her hands together, took them apart again. 'Look, Henry, I think it's time, I mean the children are growing up, education is not just a matter of going to school and reading books, it is a question of home environment etcetera and all the, you know, things a parent can do to help, and I realize you try very hard, but when you come right down to it, it is a practical business of making sure they have, how shall I put it, a background of accurate *facts* and reliable information, and, I do hope I'm not putting this badly, it is a bit embarrassing, but what I am trying to say is –'

Fickling raised his hand, closed his eyes, smiled.

'I know what you're driving at, Doreen,' he said, 'and there is no need to be embarrassed. I have already been giving the matter much thought, not to mention explaining one or two of the basics to Nigel, to wit, how Father Bee lies down beside Mother Bee and puts ovary in

51

her stamen and so forth, but I think it went over his head a bit. Nevertheless –'

'Oh, God,' murmured Doreen Fickling.

'What?'

'That wasn't actually what I was talking about, Henry,' she said. 'What I was attempting to point out was –'

The doorbell chimed.

'Yes?' enquired Fickling.

'I'm from *Encyclopaedia Britannica*,' said the young man.

'There's no Greeks here,' said Fickling.

'I'm sorry?'

'*I'm* not,' snapped Fickling. 'Come over here and throwing yourselves on your husband's bonfires, it's not bloody natural. I believe you sit on the floor to have tea, am I right?'

The young man glanced at the address on his clipboard, and at the number beside the bell, and back at Fickling.

'I don't understand,' he said.

'Bloody hell,' sighed Fickling, 'you'd think they'd have a few basic phrases before they got on the boat, is it any wonder we have got out of the Common Market? Look, Ali,' he said, 'you – have – das – wrongo – house. Compree?'

'Is this not the Fickling residence?'

Henry Fickling narrowed his eyes, but nodded.

'Then,' said the young man, 'these are yours.'

Whereupon he turned and hurried down the path, leaving Fickling staring at a large wooden packing-case. He dragged it inside.

'They've come, then,' said his wife.

'Come?' said Fickling. 'What have?'

'I tried to tell you,' she said.

So she told him now.

He did not, however, lose his temper, as she had feared. Instead, he put his hand on her shoulder.

'I blame myself, Doreen,' he said. 'You tried to warn

me and, like Nelson, I put the microscope in my wrong ear. I have clearly neglected my parental responsibility. From now on, I shall put myself at the disposal of their enquiring little minds whenever they need assistance. I am touched that you should have taken the trouble to purchase these, but I have little doubt that there is an eager market for an unused set at a generous discount. There must be a lot of dim bastards about, keen to improve themselves.'

'But –'

· 'No bother at all, my love. It is merely a matter of knocking out an eye-catching advert and popping it in the *Sunday Times*. Won't take me a moment.'

At which, taking up the pad and pencil that lay beside the phone, he jotted where he stood.

'There!' he cried. 'That'll pull 'em in.'

She looked at it.

'I always thought Britannica was with one t and two n's,' she said.

Fickling smiled tolerantly.

'Yes,' he said, 'a lot of people make that mistake.'

Straight Man

W.H. Foskett: The Life of a Bloke
Eric Breene Mullins £7.95

On a simmering June day in 1913, when the subject of this riveting new biography was only six, his mother, Isadora Foskett, returned unexpectedly from a shopping expedition to nearby Willesden. Without warning, she walked into her bedroom in the comfortable family villa Erzanmine. Her son, Wystan Hugh Foskett, was standing in front of her full-length mirror.

He was wearing men's clothes.

Still numb with shock, Isadora wrote to her sister two days later:

> 'Wystan seemed utterly unashamed. He turned somewhat awkwardly in his father's galoshes, and bowed stiffly. His bowler hat fell off.
>
>   I did not know what to say then, nor do I now. As you know, we had hoped he would one day join Diaghilev, or change the face of English poetry, or compose grand opera, or revolutionize economics. Certainly, he has manifested a talent for all this, and more. But now, I suppose, he will have to go into Foskett's Depilatory Soups.'

She was foolish enough not to mention the incident to the boy's headmaster; biographer Breene suggests that she may have hoped that young Wystan would grow out of it. Had she informed the school of his strange sexual predisposition, they might have been prepared to bend the rules; as it was, when the headmaster took the boy on his lap a few weeks later in order to audition him for the part of Hedda Gabler, Wystan bit him on the hand.

He was asked to leave St Bosie's and, over the next few years, a further dozen of the better prep schools. In 1919, however, he managed to scrape into Eton, despite the fact that his lips were considered too thin, on the strength of the Chanel No. 5 which his desperate mother had managed to squirt into his hair on the morning of the interview. But, inevitably, he was unhappy there: Breene quotes this piece of juvenilia, composed in 1923:

> *'The first XV are dancing in the showers,*
> *The Classics Sixth are trying on their pearls;*
> *The Racquets Club have been at it for hours,*
> *While I sit here, alone, and dream of girls.'*

Only once did Foskett's stubborn pursuit of the love that dare not speak its name work to his advantage. In the 1920s, girls bobbed their hair, flattened their chests, and smoked black stogies; and when Foskett took a young Slough barmaid on a trip to Oxford in 1925 and (needing to kill time until nightfall, when he planned to defile a punt) walked into Christ Church with what the dons took to be a youth in false eyelashes and a bee-sting mouth, he was offered a scholarship on the spot.

Oxford in 1925, Mr Breene vividly reminds us for the ninety-third time, was entering a Golden Era; and Foskett, determined now to be a poet, rejoiced at the proximity of Auden, Spender, Harold Acton, A.L. Rowse, Louis Macneice, Tom Driberg, Richard Crossman, and, of course, Christopher Isherwood, who, although at Cambridge, spent most of his time in Oxford following the expansion of Morris Motors at Cowley, which had brought thousands of rough young mechanics flooding thither from all over England.

When Auden invited him to a party in Peck Quad, Foskett was overjoyed. He took along a sheaf of his imagist poems and (since the card had suggested he bring a dear friend) Miss Doreen Nugent, who trimmed seats for bullnose Morris tourers and was reputed to be able to crack walnuts with her bust. What followed is poignantly described by the young poet in a letter to Stanley Tibbs, an Ealing glazier.

'As I stepped into the room, Auden sprang forward eagerly to greet me; but upon spotting Miss Nugent behind me, he let out a small cry, and fell back into the arms of C. Day Lewis, who, attempting to revive Auden by mouth-to-mouth resuscitation, was kicked in the head by a jealous Isherwood. A terrible silence fell upon the room; Driberg and Crossman stood frozen in mid-tango, unable to take their eyes from Miss Nugent.

As to what happened next, I cannot be clear. It may have been Nijinsky who hit me with the table-lamp, and Miss Nugent thinks that the people who threw her out of the window were all Sitwells, but neither of us can be sure. I know only that I woke up in the Isis, with my poems floating illegibly around me.'

Disillusioned with Oxford, aware that his poetry would find no market there (the editor of *Isis*, meeting him two days later in the High, felled him with his reticule), Foskett left the university at the end of the term and went to Austria to write a novel. He was never to finish it; pursued from *gasthaus* to *gasthaus* by lust-crazed peasant youths who had heard that he was an English writer, he managed to escape across the Brenner Pass into Switzerland on the night of September 5, 1927, disguised as a St Bernard. Only one fragment of his writing remains from this period, quoted by Breene:

'*Lederhosen suffuse my nightmares;*
Knees close in.
I choke on hat-feathers.'

His time in Switzerland, however, was far from happy.

His father having died, W.H. Foskett inherited a hundred thousand pounds, which enabled him to stay at the Palace in Gstaad, where André Gide, having recently sold the US rights of *Les Faux-Monnayeurs*, had taken the bridal suite. Every day, from its balcony, Gide scanned the nursery slopes through his binoculars, and upon catching sight of Wystan's large-brimmed felt hat one morning, he let out an impassioned shriek and set off in hot pursuit.

Despite the fact that Gide's skis wore out at Domodossola, the terrified Foskett kept going until he reached Venice. It was not the wisest of moves. Most of Bloomsbury was in Venice that year, and spending money lavishly on local goods; Wystan Foskett being the only English heterosexual in the enchanted city, whenever he accepted a ride from the horde of clamouring gondoliers he would find himself swimming back across the filthy Grand Canal, pursued by jeers, his knuckles bruised, his sensibilities shredded.

Lytton Strachey, however, took pity on him; at least, initially. Strachey had gone to Venice to finish a sentence, with money given to him by Duncan Grant who had won it from Clive Bell in a bet concerning a personal habit of J.M. Keynes so peculiarly illegal that even now, fifty years on, biographer Breene is not permitted to describe it. Having toyed with his sentence for five weeks and reached, at last, a convenient comma, Strachey felt he deserved a month off; and, encountering the dripping Foskett as he splashed wretchedly ashore at St Mark's Square for the twentieth time, Strachey offered him a glass of strega and a quick tour of the Doge's palace. Foskett was at first suspicious; but so enervated had Lytton become by his industry (he had written over fourteen words), that every time he reached out to touch Wystan when the corridors took a darker turn, his hand merely fell back limply to his side.

They thus contracted, perforce, a Platonic friendship; and upon his return to London, Foskett, his novel now finished, rushed straight round to the apartment of the man who had promised to bring his enormous influence to bear in its publication.

The extracts quoted from memory by Breene show it to have been a major advance in English fiction; had it been published, there is no question but that the entire subsequent course of English letters would have been radically different. In the event, however, E.M. Forster was in Strachey's bath when Foskett called and sprang at the young visitor with such force that Lytton, two rooms away, fell off the milkman. Rushing out into the street in panic, Foskett was knocked down by a bus. When he woke up, two days later, in St George's Hospital, his manuscript had vanished.

That was in 1929. For the next two or three years, Wystan Foskett lived from hand to mouth, working on his writing but shunned by the literary establishment, the very depths of which were by now penetrated by scandalous rumours of his sexual habits. He had been spotted at the Locarno, Streatham, it was said, dancing with a woman; he had left, apparently, a glittering literary banquet at the very moment when the most respected publisher in London had suggested that everyone swap bras; it was even suggested that he might be getting engaged.

As the result of this ostracism, Foskett penned what Breene considers his major verse work, *The Ascent of F All*, a bitter, pessimistic epic, inadvertently burnt by Foskett's agent in a fit of pique after Sir Maurice Bowra had spurned his advances. All that remains is the charred extract shown in the photograph on page 98, from which Breene formed, in my view correctly, his appreciative judgement.

Understandably soured by the appalling circumstances of his persecution, Foskett, now 25, decided to give up literature altogether. There was also a political motive for this decision; Foskett had gone to Germany in 1932, and had been deeply shocked by what he had seen. The lakes were full of naked Nazis; observing their behaviour on beaches and in beer-halls, Wystan Foskett formed the opinion that if Hitler ever realized his dream, all heterosexuals would be exterminated. When Hitler assumed power in 1933, Foskett pledged himself to fighting the Nazi sexual menace; he became a Communist, and went up to Cambridge to learn Russian.

He allowed his political persuasion to become known, in the hope of thereby making contact with courageous and decent men who might be encouraged to recruit him as a Russian agent; he would thus be able to work for the overthrow of the Nazi regime at a time when Britain herself seemed pledged only to compromise, appeasement, and ultimately subordination.

On November 9, 1933, he found a note in his pigeon hole, requesting his presence at a room in Trinity. Excitedly, that evening he went along. In the room were Guy Burgess, Kim Philby, Donald MacLean and Anthony Blunt.

When he emerged from the room two hours later, his eyes, according to an ancient Trinity porter discovered in Newmarket by Breene, were strangely glazed. He walked to his digs without a word, packed, left Cambridge the next morning and went to London. That afternoon, he joined the Blackshirts.

For nearly three years thereafter, Wystan Foskett dedicated himself to the cause; but while his colleagues were down in Stepney fighting Jews, Foskett chose instead to hang around Russell Square with a pick-handle, felling anyone who came out of Faber & Faber. Then, in July 1936, the Spanish Civil War broke out, and Foskett, as his biographer poignantly tells it in the final moving chapters, rushed to join up.

And there it was, in the proud ranks of the Condor Legion, that the restless and persecuted spirit of W.H. Foskett found at last its fulfilment, and its rest. By mid-1937, he had earned the Iron Cross and the Blue Max with crossed palms and oak-leaves, and been personally congratulated by Franco. Renowned for the pin-point accuracy of his dive-bombing, it was this, ironically, for which he finally paid the ultimate price: it was on a mission to bomb W.H. Auden that Foskett's Stuka was tragically, on August 17, shot down.

There were no literary figures at his funeral. But eighty-seven women turned up, to weep and to provide, in Breene's telling final words, 'a testament to one English writer's bizarre priorities'.

In a Little Spanish Town

*Although the ETA threat must not be minimised, it is
our experience that the British holidaymaker in particular takes such things very stoically. And, of course,
our hoteliers are going out of their way to reassure guests
by every possible means. Most people will notice nothing
out of the ordinary at all.*
        Spanish Tourist Authority spokesman, on BBC

                      Hotel Perdicion,
                      Las Ruinas,
                      Costa Brava.
                      Wednesday

Dear Auntie Doreen,
    Well, here we are in viva espana as we say down here,
olay, olay, and the sun coming down a treat, Kevin's head
is already wrinkled like pork crackling and unable to
wear free hat but never mind, it will come in useful as an
oven glove, not his head, the hat, thank God he had
Bakofoil round his conk is all I can say, he's a sullen
bugger when he's peeling, I remember last year in, I
think it was Crete, the place where they have sardine
dances anyway, I remember last year when flakes kept
falling off his nose into the soup, there was no living
with him, all them long silences, I can see him now
sitting up in bed all night, glowing like that thing on the
bottom of the freezer, pilot light is it?
    I thought he was going to get upset on our first day,
mind, when there was this big bang and our balcony
blew off, he'd hung his Aertex shirt on it to dry the

armpits out on account of us having to stay four hours in
the airport bus due to mines being dug out of the road in
front, but it wasn't as bad as it sounds, they give us free
oranges and a colouring book for the kids which Kevin
said would have cost he reckoned over a pound in the
shops, only trouble was little Darryl drew on the woman
in front with his felt-tip and there was a bit of a row, her
going on about sitting down to dinner with PIS OFF
ARSNEL on her back. They come and told us the mines
had been put in the road due to clerical error and Kevin
said typical.

Anyway, he went out on the balcony, or where the
balcony would have been, and naturally said where's my
bleeding leisurewear etc, but the manager come up and
said he was terribly sorry, they were celebrating the forty-
second anniversary of nearly the end of the Spanish Civil
War and a firework had fallen off the roof, and Kevin
replied quick as a flash, no wonder he's popular up
Standard Telephones & Cables, Kevin replied first I've
heard of celebrating anything by blowing up somebody's
shirt!

Well, the manager took his point, that is what they're
paid for after all, and he was back in two minutes with a
brand new floral shirt, very sheek, it's sort of a yellow, I
suppose you'd call it, with these cocktail glasses all over
it, Kevin looks like Ryan O'Neal in it except for his head
of course.

Lucky he was not wearing it for dinner that night, is
all I can say! He had fortunately changed into an old
white one you can drip dry over the bath because you
know what foreign food is like with sauces and so forth, I
remember one year we went to Italy or somewhere,
anyway you have to go by coach, and they give us this big
plate of spaghetti absolutely *swimming* in tomato sauce
and within ten minutes Kevin had to take his No-Glu
Hairpiece off, in front of everybody, because, as he went
to some length to point out, they do not make them from
real human hair so you have to get them dry-cleaned, and
it probably cost a fortune in Italy and suppose they lost

it? He got most of the meat out with his serviette, but it smelt of garlic all that winter, people kept moving away up the bingo.

So he was wearing his old white shirt as a precaution, and he must be psychic, because one minute he was looking at his paiella and next minute it had exploded, there was bits of prawn everywhere. Naturally, he called the waiter across and said Oy, I never bloody ordered this, did I, and the head waiter came over and apologized and said there had been a mix-up in the kitchen and brought him double egg chips and beans, and Kevin said that's a bit more bloody like it. He doesn't like making a fuss, but you have to show these people who's boss, after all, it's not as if you weren't paying for it.

Darryl and Tracy and Sharon all had the fish finger special and were sick all over the lift afterwards, which was particularly embarrassing for Sharon, being fourteen and with a big bust due to being on the pill, girls are sensitive at that age, and the manager calling the doctor only made matters worse, his hands were all over her, I don't think they have the same medical ethics in Spain, if he done it at home he'd have been in the *Sun*, anyway he said whatever it was it was definitely not rat poison in the batter, any talk of rat poison was idle gossip, he would personally stake his reputation on the fact that none of it was due to rat poison. After he'd gone Kevin said typical, they probably want us to think it's rat poison to disguise the fact that it was their lousy cooking, he would ask for a refund at the earliest opportunity, he did not call haute cuisine something that ended up on the floor of a lift. Not much gets past Kevin!

They brought us breakfast in bed next morning, and I said that's nice, Kevin, and Kevin said hang about, we never asked for this, I bet there's a room service charge, and then the waiter pulled a knife out, and Kevin said what did I tell you, he only wants a bloody tip on top of it! But the waiter said no he didn't, he was a free Basque and we were his hostages, and Kevin said sod that, this holiday was costing £159 a head not to mention deckchairs also six hours in Gatwick due to baggage-handlers' strike and would the waiter care to step out on the balcony and discuss it, so the waiter stepped out onto where the balcony was before the firework blew it off and he fell fifteen floors into the car park, and Kevin said next year it's Clacton, definitely.

But he cheered up on the beach. He's never been one for the beach, nothing to do he says except keep washing stuff off your feet, but there was some sort of local folk thing on like the time we were in, is Morocco the one I brought you back the clock from, where the cuckoo falls out, anyway it was sort of like that, Kevin and me and everybody else had to sit behind this barbed wire they've got, and there was people with Napoleon type hats on at one end in holes in the sand and a lot of other people in overalls at the other end, and they all had machine-guns. The manager came out with a tin hat on and a megaphone and said it was all being done for a film, and Kevin said stone me, it's bloody realistic, that bloke's head's just come off, but the kids liked it, except Darryl, who had a hole shot through his Mickey Mouse bucket and his crab got out, and Kevin said bloody kids, typical, always complaining about something, a hundred-and-fifty-nine quid, but he smacked Darryl's head and felt better.

Due to the kitchen burning down unexpected we had to have cold meat and Kevin said sometimes this bloody country amazes me, they do everything here with bloody onions except pickle them, typical. If I was Sarsons I'd open a factory here, you could clean up. He's always been full of good commercial ideas, as you know, but his view is, what's the point of making a million, they don't let you keep it, don't talk to me about bloody governments. The way Kevin sees right through things is uncanny sometimes.

Like the business with Sharon after lunch. This little Spaniard come up while we was having what they call a siesta by the Watney's stand and he shoved this note in Kevin's hand and ran off. Kevin looked at it and informed yours truly what it said: we have got your daughter, signed ETA. So I said who's ETA and Kevin informed me that he did not bloody know, but he was going to ask the manager, and when he came back he said the manager had told him it stood for English Tourist Authority and they often came and took girls off for a bit and gave them a good time, it was all part of Anglo-Spanish relations etcetera and he'd tell Kevin more about it sometime when he wasn't quite so busy, he had to go now and see about repairing the telephone wires, they had all been cut due to gulls pecking through them.

So Kevin went back to sleep, and next thing we knew there was Sharon waking us up saying could she have a hundred pesetas for a coke, she had just been raped and it made her thirsty. And I said raped? raped? what do you mean raped? and Sharon said it was something they did in Spain, it was like Charlie Matthews next door, only quicker. So Kevin gave her the money, and after she'd gone he said all I seem to do is bloody shell out, if she's in pod I'll sue that bloody pill company, I'm not spending a fortune on prams etcetera at my age. If that's what the English Tourist Authority calls entertainment, it's a bloody disgrace, she can get all that at home, why didn't they take her on a pedalo?

Whizz for Atomms

'*Molesworth chosen as cruise missile site*' – Guardian

The scene is the dark, doom-haunted skool of st. custards chiz chiz moan drone where the tiny pupils live a life of friteful sufering at the hands of the headmaster **GRIMES** and his band of thugs who have the impertence to call themselves masters.

Our hero dashing **NIGEL MOLESWORTH** hem hem is stroling the dank flagstoans his hansome brow furroed in thought his lithe yung muscles bunched like a traned panther. O wot can ale thee, knite at arms? cry **FOTHERINGTON-TOMAS**, the skool gurly. Our hero lash out with left jab folloed by right upercut, hurra hurra scream packed masses in madison square gardn, but FOTHERINGTON-TOMAS meerly nip behind MATRON's skurt, shreeking 'Wot dredfull thing hav got into Molesworth, matron, he is normly the most humain of men help help!'

MATRON clasp trembling weed to mitey boosum (tuf luck think our hero it is hel in there!) and sa:

'Leeve Nigel aloan, deer, he hav cleerly sufered major shock as we sa in medical proffeshun, perhaps he need enema etc. poaked up him, har har, cum along Nigel, snap out of it, dont do that it wil make yore nose big it will gro warts on yore appendix yu will go blind etc etc.'

MATRON and FOTHERINGTON-TOMAS woddle off cacklin like ugly duckling plus barmy mater, leaving solitry figur gaizing into bleek futur. They cleerly hav not read toda's gardian notised by our hero as it go by beneeth arm of SIGISMUND the mad maths master, SIGISMUND is tipical gardian reeder ie uterly barmy, he cri free al wimmen, he cri free al politickle prisners, he cri free al hostiges, he cri free al medisine etc, only thing SIGISMUND not cri is free al tiny pupils held against there wil by mad maths masters, act now and end this cruel and filthy fashist oppreshun in name of democrasy etc.

Anyway, their it was in blak and wite as mmm lope past: MOLESWORTH CHOSEN AS CRUISE MIS- SILE SITE. At this feerful news, our hero reeled, wurld swam befor his yung eyes, hole life flashd in front of him! Mother of God is this the end of molesworth? cri the striken figur, eckoing Famous Last Wurds of e g robbinson in litl caesar as seen at skool cinma club (tho wot e g robbinson hav in comon with caesar is beyond yore correspondant, e g robbinson hav not climed hils to look for winter quarters, e g robbinson hav not set up camps on this side of the rivr and also on that, e g robbinson hav not dispatched labienus to seek pro- visions ere nite fall etc etc).

Hardlie hav MATRON and FOTHERINGTON- TOMAS been swollowed up by the dismal murke than a new cloud appear on horizon no bigr than a mans fist, in the shape of PEASON chiz chiz. PEASON is knone to histry as molesworths best friend e.g. TONTO, PRINCE FILIP, STARRSKY etc etc, and their is no dout he hav many valuable qualities such as dead shot with ink dart, master forger of sik noats ('n. molesworth wil not be able to atend cros-country run as he hav sustaned majer hart attak, sined MATRON'), but it canot be sed of him that he is a simpathetic eer in times of trouble e.g. when yu hav just been seleckted as furst strike RUSIAN target chiz chiz chiz.

PEASONS reaction to news is tipical i.e. he fall down and role about larfing immodrately. When he recover, he sa: 'That is life molesworth, one must lern to take the ruf with the smooth, ours not to reeson why, into each life a litl rane must fall, i do not think i need to draw a picture, yu win a few yu lose a few etc etc..'

'Ha!' i reposte, quik as a flash. 'i think that if it was a question of a litl rane falling on me i would not be found wanting, peason, but wot we are deeling with here is a pre-emptiv nuclear strike. After a pre-emptiv nuclear strike i.e. SOVIET UNION v NIGEL MOLESWORTH, it wil not be a matter of hanging mi clothes in front of the fire to dry, peason, it wil be a matter of farewell molesworth thou art too deer for our posessing as the bard hav it.'

At this, PEASON gro grave.

'This will mean that yu have to leave st. custards, molesworth,' he sa. 'Their wil be a wip-round for a digtal watch or something. It comes at a bad moment in the term for me, i may have to owe yu for a bit.' Sudenly his fase britened. 'Of course, if their was a nuclear attak on yu befor I had managed to setle my debts, i do not suppose yore people wuld press the matter. I have met yore pater and he seemed a desent sort, if a trifle comon.'

i stair at him Fixedly.

'i do not see why i shuld hav to leave the skool,' i sa.

'As i understand it,' reply peason, 'it did not sa in the gardian that *st. custards* was chosen as the cruise missile site. The headmaster may be, and i quoat, a monster of calous cruelty who fly into a bate at every oportunity, but that does not mean he envisiges winning Wurld War Three on the playing-feilds of st. custards. GRIMES does not strike me as a man who wuld litely giv up an income of sevral milion pounds a term.' He put his hand on my shoulder. 'Yu wil hav to go off on yore own to be a missile site, nigel, far from human habitashun and liv on roots and beries etc etc.'

'Wot is this i hear?' cri a familiar voice. 'molesworth leeving us?'

It is none other than GRABBER, head of the skool, admired by al, and winner of every prize, including the mrs joyful prize for rafia work! i look up into grabbers inteligent but kindly fase, and explane the grimm facts.

grabbers brows nit.

'Dulce et decorum est pro patria mori,' sa grabber gently.

i look at peason.

'i think it is something about ice-cream for yore father,' sa peason. GRABBER grin tolrantly. He is strikt but fare.

'It mean,' he mermer, 'that their is no finer thing for a chap to do than lay down his life for his country. Yu hav been chosen, molesworth, and yu must be proud.'

'Why me, GRABBER?' i inquire, since grabber hav a giant grasp of international affares etc etc.

'wel,' sa grabber, 'let me try to make it as simpl as posible. When Wurld War Three brakes out, molesworth, it wil not be wot we call holesale war immediately. It wil start off convenshenal, ie it wil take the rusians up to three days to shove nato into the sea, using there eight billion tanks etc. America will then sa: this canot go on, we shal hav to use nuclear wepons chiz chiz all that money down the drane.'

'is that when they let off the things round molesworth?' inquire PEASON eegerly.

'Yes,' repli grabber. 'It is quite sensibl really, if tuf on molesworth. Yu see, molesworth do not hav wot we call stragetic importance, he is not a majer populashun centre, he is not a military instalashun, he is not a prime minister or archbishep or queen etc, he is meerly a smorl boy sitting on topp of a load of missiles. He is wot we call a token target. It is my guess that their is a simlar smorl boy on the rusian side, let us cal him for arguments sake MOLESWORTHSKI, a tipical ie farely dim tiny pupil at st. custardovs, a prep skool in the dreer waists of siberia. The americans wil let off there molesworth missiles and blarst molesworthski and his site to smithereens, wearupon the rusians wil say aha! this is stage two as lade down in the Big War Book, and imediately fire off *there* nuclear missiles and uterly wipe out the molesworth (UK) site!'

'including molesworth?' inquire PEASON, simpath-etically piking his nose.

'Yes,' sa GRABBER, 'i am afraid so.'

peason shrug his shoulders.

'It needn't be so bad,' he sa comfortingly. 'With any luck, yu wil go to Hel, yu can muk about al day and burn things and stik wite-hot forks up people and shreek foul othes etc etc. As a matter of fact,' the swine continue, 'i quite envy yu.'

'Yes,' add grabber, 'also yu will hav the honor of being the first st. custards boy to be wiped out in a nuclear attak, yu wil go on the rol of honor just like al the st. custards boys who died in World War One and World War Two, it wil be jolly nise for your people on poppy day knowing they have done there bit etc etc.'

At this, our hero do nothing. n. molesworth is not one to blubb openly. Instead, he meerly smile the sikly smile of one who know his number is upp.

'Hurra!' cri molesworth, albeit weekly.

'Yes,' grabber go on, 'and another thing, remember that the molesworth missile site wil bring much-needed trade to the area.'

'Wot do yu mean?' inquire the galant subjekt of this tale.

'It is a phrase yu see al the time,' explane grabber. 'yu

are probably a bit yung to understand al the implic-
ations, but wot it mean in prinsiple is that while the
americans are putting up the missiles round yu etc etc, yu
wil get chewing-gum coka-cola cheesbergers comiks
donald duk tea-shirts and so forth and they wil spend a
lot of dollars on local pubs and local gurls hem hem, it is
called economics.'

our hero nod sagely.

'i see,' he repli. 'And after I hav been blarsted, wot
happens to the War then?'

'Wel,' sa the all-knowing grabber, perl of his
generashun, 'everyone wil come and stair at the hole etc
and sa: so thats wot happens when you drop nuclear
boms on people, wel wel, i think we ought to stopp it rite
now befor somebody reely important gets hurt.'

'such as?' inquire peason.

'such as Americans,' sa grabber.

Darling Greengrocer ...

THE COREN LETTERS

Alan Coren was possibly one of the last great letter writers. Certainly, he was greater than Evelyn Waugh, if only because he was forced to labour under the disadvantage that nobody ever wrote to him; since, by 1980, postal costs had come to prohibit anything but commercial mail. Nevertheless, Coren toiled on, confident in the belief that it was still the cheapest way of cobbling together a big fat book.

To Lex Volvo (UK) Ltd.

(5 February 1980)

My dear Lex: I cannot thank you enough for your delightfully entertaining bill! Were dear Tom Driberg still alive, I have little doubt but that he would have been as thrilled as I to discover that it is still possible, despite the assorted plights which rack this unfortunate island, to have the rear door of a shooting brake (why, oh why, do the appalling little swine who presently hold the culture in thrall insist upon calling them *estates*? Have they any conception of what is conjured up in the mind of a gentleman by the words *Volvo Estate* – some appalling Scandinavian tract with snow upon the croquet lawn and unutterably boring Swedes falling off horses while their suicidal footmen slit throats in the freezing buttery?), to have the rear door of a shooting brake, I say, beaten out, sprayed up to customer's specifications, refitted, and made good for as little as £367.55, to include new wipe-wash motor.

I passed another somewhat wretched evening yesterday. I went along to Boodle's, and was involved in a bit of a row. Apparently one has to be a member to get in.

To Maxwell House

(3 March 1980)

Good old Max! I received your enchanting letter in the post this morning, and confess myself overwhelmed by your astonishingly generous offer.

And yet, and yet. How am I to reply without appearing the charmless boor that society chooses so often to represent me as? I truly cannot get away to the sunsoaked Balkan Riviera this year, even if I had the half-dozen 8oz lids you mention or could think of the three words necessary to complete your sentence. Can you forgive me? The plain fact of the matter is, I have a great deal on my plate at the moment – do you know Lex Volvo? No matter, it is a long and dispiriting tale, but the top and bottom of it is that he has dealt with me rather badly for an old acquaintance. My new rear door does not shut properly, and when I bang it hard, the little lights fall out of that thing over the number plate. I fear a frightful row may be brewing between us, and I dare not leave London until it is settled. You know how people are.

Once again, dear Max, my thanks and apologies. I am delighted to hear that your new granules are twenty per cent tastier. God knows, good news is rare enough, these days.

To his Greengrocer

(5 March 1980)

Darling Greengrocer: Thank you so much for the wonderful sprouts! Your boy hurried round last evening and pressed them into my hand personally – was it only fancy that made the little brown bag still warm from your own hand?

They could not have arrived at a more opportune time. I had been feeling very depressed all day, what with one thing and another; I had to turn down dear old Max's offer of a free trip to the Crimea, and immediately after that, not only did the little lights fall out of that thing over the number plate again, but the new rear windscreen wiper failed to wipe the new rear windscreen. What do you suppose Lex is playing at, after all these years? And as if all *that* were not enough, I was cut dead upon Hampstead Heath by a woman who might very well have been the Duchess of Argyll. Is she a tall woman with a purple conk?

In any event, your sprouts were a marvellous surprise. I had been expecting 5lb King Edwards, 2lb Williams pears, and a small turnip.

P.S. My new book, to make matters yet worse, is going very badly. I am stuck on page 23. Can I be alone in finding Margaret Drabble unreadable?

To Lex Volvo

(7 March 1980)

Dear Volvo: My curtness only reflects your own. I was appalled this morning to receive from you a *printed acknowledgement*, one month late, of my letter of February 5th [*see above. Ed.*].

Not that I am altogether surprised. I have noticed of late an entirely, to me, inexplicable change of attitude on your part towards the cavalier and uncaring. It may interest you to know (though, upon reflection, I rather doubt it, given your new unconcern) that I was so distressed by the little lights falling out of that thing over the number plate that I was forced to give up a much-needed holiday with Max.

I have twice this past week driven over to your place in the hope of seeing you and perhaps persuading you to glance at my inert wash-wipe mechanism, but on both occasions your man informed me that an appointment was necessary. An *appointment*? Between *us*?

I confess I do not know what is happening to society. London is full of both Jews and Arabs. Sainsbury's, one's grocers, is like a soukh. I beg leave, for both our sakes, to suggest that this general erosion of all that is good and decent may be what lies behind your own coolness to me; were your behaviour none of your own choice but merely the contamination of this ghastly world, I should be greatly reassured, though nonetheless low in spirit.

To the Scottish Widows Insurance Society
(10 March 1980)

Dear, dear Ladies! Words cannot adequately express my gratitude for your kind card. That it fell out of one's *Reader's Digest*, like a bolt from the blue, instead of being thrust through one's letter box crumpled by one of those black hooligans who these days, such is our national decline, bear the sacred mission of Her Majesty's mail, made it even more welcome.

Alas, how can I accept your offer of £7,642 for me at age 65? Granted that the inflation visited upon our aching backs by a succession of governments each more villainously corrupt than the last must have, by now, ensured that the mite stands considerably higher than its AD 33 value, how on earth would you manage to scrape together this considerable sum over the next quarter century? How, indeed, could I commit your twilight years to scrimping and self-denial simply in order to bring a measure of security to an ageing hack?

That cannot be. Nevertheless, your rare charity in this beastly world shines like a beacon. You are obviously Roman Catholics, and I thank God that you and your line have been spared the poisonous taint of the heretical Knox and thus saved from the stinking sulphur and flaying agonies of the spit-roasted hell into which he and all who slobber after his maniacal ravings are irredeemably doomed to hurtle.

To his Greengrocer
(11 March 1980)

Dear Chas. Rumbold & Son: I am deeply distressed by a

visit I have just received, during an afternoon I had intended giving over to thinking about my relationship with Lady Diana Mosley, should we ever meet, by two persons to whom I should not have given an audience had their boots not been wedged in my front door.

Thus to reply to my affectionate letter of March 5th only serves to strengthen my conviction that England is truly finished. As I told your repugnant minions after I had got up again, my erstwhile affection for you was entirely platonic, nor have I ever laid a finger on Brian, your delivery boy. If any blame attaches to me, it is in assuming that by treating tradesmen as equals, gentlemen might perhaps offer them the chance of rising above the mire in which they clearly prefer to wallow.

And before my observations prompt you to further outrage, reflect upon this; one of your sprouts, it transpired, had a worm in it.

To Lex Volvo

(15 March 1980)

Dear Volvo: Following a further printed travesty suggesting that I telephone, and I quote, *one of your service staff* for an appointment (*Author's italics. Ed.*), it occurs to me that this shocking behaviour can have but one explanation. Are you yourself a Swede? If so, together with my deepest commiseration, I take the liberty of enclosing a humble little card from some Scottish widows of my acquaintance in order to demonstrate to you that there remain a few isolated pockets in this ugly and malevolent world where good manners and unrapacious hearts yet continue, albeit feebly, to flourish.

Getting the Hump

A suit of armour sold last week for £1,850 is believed to have been worn by King Richard III. It had been tailor-made for a man 5ft 4ins tall with a curvature of the spine and one shoulder lower than the other. – Sunday Express

Although, on the morning of April 6, 1471, the bright spring sun may have been warming the narrow London streets and cheering the spirits of the teeming citizens, its heartening rays unfortunately penetrated neither the dank and tatty premises of Master Sam Rappaport (Bespoke Metal Tailoring Since 1216) Ltd, nor the sunken soul of its hapless proprietor.

Master Rappaport had staff shortages. True, Rappaport's had had staff shortages ever since that fateful day in 1290, but this week was particularly bad: his vambrace cutter was off sick, his hauberk finisher was in labour, and the heads of his two best riveters were currently shrivelling on the north gate of London Bridge for dishonestly handling a church roof which they had hoped to turn into a natty spring range of lead leisurewear.

'So ask me where I'm getting gauntlets from!' he demanded bitterly of his senior assistant, as he walked through the door.

The senior assistant sighed; but it was what he was paid for, mainly, so he said:

'Okay, Sam, so where are you getting gauntlets from?'

'Don't ask!' snapped his master.

The senior assistant summoned his dutiful laugh, for the thousandth time.

'Gauntlets I'm buying off the peg, thank God my poor father never lived to see it,' muttered Master Rappaport. 'A man walks out of here in what he thinks are genuine hand-forged Rappaport gauntlets, he goes into a tavern for a glass of sherry wine, he bangs his fist on the table, and what is he looking at?'

'What?'

'Flat fingers, is what he's looking at. A webbed hand, is what he's looking at. Tin is all they are. Time was, a man in a Rappaport gauntlet, he wanted to shake hands, he needed two other people to help him lift.'

The shop-bell jangled.

A tall good-looking young man filled the doorway.

'Good morrow,' he said. 'I am the Duke of Gloucester.'

Master Rappaport turned bitterly to his senior assistant.

'See?' he snapped. 'I ask for underpressers, they send me dukes!'

'I think he's a customer, Sam,' murmured the senior assistant.

The grey preoccupation ebbed from Master Rappaport's face. He smacked his forehead. He banged his breast. He bowed.

'Forgive me, Your Grace!' he cried. 'How may we assist you?'

'I should like,' said the Duke of Gloucester, 'a suit of armour. Nothing flash, and plenty of room in the seat.'

The master tailor beamed.

'Wonderful!' he said. 'Formal, but also informal, smart for day wear, but if God forbid you should suddenly have to kill somebody at night, you don't want to be embarrassed, am I right?'

'You read my mind, sir!' cried the young Duke.

'I have been in this game a long time,' said Master Rappaport. 'Nat, the swatches!'

The senior assistant bustled across with a number of clanking plates gathered on a loop of chain. Master Rappaport flicked over them.

'Not the toledo,' he murmured, mostly to himself, 'toledo is all right on an older man, it's a heavyweight, it's fine if you don't have to run around too much, also the sheffield, personally I got nothing against sheffield, it has a smart glint, but you have to be short, there's nothing worse than a long glint, believe me; likewise, the cast-iron, a tall man in cast-iron, he can look like a walking stove. For my money, I see you in the non-iron.'

'Non-iron?'

'It's a synthetic, 20% copper, a bit of this, a bit of that; a lightweight, wonderful for summer battles. A lot of people couldn't get away with it, but you're young, you got broad shoulders, a nice figure, you can carry a thinner metal. It's flexible, it's cool, it don't creak suddenly when you're with – hem! hem! – a young lady, you should forgive my presumption. Also got a lightweight fly, just a little snap catch, very convenient; the cast-iron, for example, it's got a big bolt it can take you all day, first thing you know you're rusting from the inside, am I right, Nat?'

'Absolutely,' said the senior assistant.

The young nobleman smiled generously.

'I shall be guided entirely by you,' he said. 'I have just returned from exile with His Majesty Edward IV, and have in consequence little notion of current fashion trends.'

'With Edward IV you've been?' cried Master Rappaport. 'So Saturday week you're fighting at Barnet?'

The Duke nodded.

'Problems, Sam?' enquired Nat, catching his master's sudden furrow.

'Eight days,' murmured his master. 'It's not long. At least three fittings he'll need.'

'Perhaps, in that case,' said the Duke, 'I ought to try –'

'We'll manage!' cried Sam Rappaport hastily, 'We'll manage! Nat, the tape!'

And, lowering his eyes respectfully, the master tailor, tape in hand, approached the comely crotch.

*

The senior assistant looked at the morning delivery. He shook his head.

'We shouldn't send the greaves out for making,' he said. 'They're a good two inches short. Also the cuisses.'

Master Rappaport stared dismally out of the little window.

'Maybe he'll agree to crouch a bit,' he said, at last. 'Look, Nat, he's been abroad, you heard him say he was out of touch. So we'll tell him all the smart crowd are crouching a bit this season. Who knows, maybe we could set a whole new –'

The bell jangled. The two tailors bowed.

'I can't get on the leg pieces without crouching,' said the young Duke, after a while, panting.

'Wonderful!' cried Sam Rappaport. 'Look at His Grace, Nat!'

'Perfect!' shouted the senior assistant. 'It fits you like the paper on the wall. This year, everybody's crouching.'

'You're sure?' enquired the anxious young man, hobbling uncomfortably before the pier-glass.

'Would I lie?' said Sam Rappaport. 'Tuesday, please God, we'll have the breastplate and pauldrons.'

'Tuesdays,' muttered the senior assistant, 'I never liked.'

They stared at the breastplate, for the tenth time. Then they measured the two shoulder pieces again.

'So we'll tell him everybody's wearing one shoulder lower this year,' said the master tailor. 'He's young, he's green, what does he know?'

'Here he is,' said Nat.

'It hurts my shoulder,' complained the Duke of Gloucester, after a minute or two. His left hand hung six inches lower than his right, his neck was strangely twisted, his legs crouched in the agonizing constrictions of the ill-made greaves and cuisses.

'Listen,' said Master Rappaport gently. 'To be fashionable, you have to suffer a bit. Is His Grace smart, Nat, or is he smart!'

'Fantastic!' cried the senior assistant, looking at the wall. 'Take my word for it, he'll be the envy of the Court.'

'When will the backplate and gorget be ready?' gasped the Duke.

'Friday,' said Master Rappaport. 'On Friday, you get the whole deal.'

'On second thoughts,' murmured the senior assistant, 'Tuesdays are a lot better than Fridays.'

'We're working under pressure!' shouted his master. 'Miracles you expect suddenly?'

He held up the backplate. It was strangely bowed, like a turtle's carapace.

'Well, gentlemen?'

They spun around. The door having been open, they had not heard the Duke come in.

'We were just admiring the backplate!' cried Master Rappaport. 'What cutting! What burnishing!'

'And what a wonderful curvature!' exclaimed Nat.

'Curvature?' enquired the Duke of Gloucester.

'It's what everybody's talking about,' said Sam.

'This time next month,' said Nat, 'everybody will be bent. I promise.'

The Duke took the finished suit to the fitting room.

Time passed. The two tailors looked at their shoes, arranged their patterns slightly, cleared their throats, looked at the ceiling.

After a few minutes, the fitting-room curtains parted, and the Duke of Gloucester slouched through, dragging his leg, swinging his long left arm, his head screwed round and pointing diagonally up.

'It looks – as though – I have – a – hump,' he managed to croak, at last, through his tortured neck.

'Thank God for that!' cried Master Rappaport. 'We were worrying, weren't we, Nat?'

'Definitely,' said the senior assistant. 'We said to ourselves: suppose the suit comes out without a fashionable hump?'

'It's killing me!' cried the Duke.

'Good!' shouted Sam.

'Wonderful!' shouted Nat.

'You're sure it's fashionable?' gasped the Duke.

'You could be a – a – a *king*!' cried Master Rappaport.

So the young Duke of Gloucester paid his bill, and, wearing his new armour, lurched horribly out into the street. And, as he walked, so the pain burned through his body; and, before very long, an unfamiliar darkness spread across his sunny face, and a new sourness entered his disposition, and angers he had never known, and rages he had never believed possible, racked the flesh beneath the steel.

And, suddenly, strangely, the world began to look a different place altogether; until, penetrating to the very innermost recesses of his soul, there fell across him on that soft spring day, a deep, black discontent, like winter.

The Holy Grail and the Holy Gravy

Despite the fact that their astounding, mindbending, faith-cracking, stunningly controversial new book about Jesus Christ is currently top of both the British and the American best-sellers lists, little is known of the authors, Wilson, Keppel, and Betty, since they have been on television only eighty-three times this week. In consequence, I decided to fly out to Zurich and interview the shy trio in their humble book-lined penthouse atop the towering Wilsonkeppelbettybank Building.

As I waited, my eyes roved, as eyes will, along the groaning shelves laden with painstakingly gathered research material; naturally, many of the titles meant nothing to a mere layman, but one or two spines in English – *The Big Boy's Book of Offshore Mutual Funds*, *The Ins and Outs of the Tokyo Bourse*, *Teach Yourself CTT Avoidance*, *A Theologian's Guide to Corporate Financing* – gave some ·small hint of the enormous amount of diligent and meticulous study into which these three gentle and retiring academics had for so long thrown themselves.

They came into the room, smiled self-effacingly, shook my hand, and counted the interview fee, before motioning me into a comfortable Eames fauteuil. Dave Wilson, at 28 the youngest of the trio, is a tall, nervous, clearly brilliant man, who almost took a top CSE in remedial raffia-work; Heinrich Keppel is a short, plump, dour Swiss accountant and thinker; and Kevin Betty, a Dagenham-born computer-programmer in his mid-thirties, likes Chinese food, *Roy of the Rovers*, and early Dickie Valentine records.

It was Kevin, in fact, who in the course of what was

hardly more than random and speculative programming first hit upon that tiny seed of truth which was, much later, to burgeon into the astonishing theory that has now set all Christendom alight.

'I could not wait to test my theory on Dave,' he told me. 'I ran all the way round to his house, only his mum said he was up Loftus Road on account of Queens Park Rangers was at home to Orient. So I tear round there, don't I? It took me ages to find him in the crowd, but eventually I did, and I grabbed hold of him and I shouted: *Dave, Dave, I think I have stumbled on sunnink which will change the whole face of Christianity as we know it!* I shall never forget his reply.'

'What did he say?' I enquired.

'He said: *Sod off, Stainrod is playing a blinder.* Didn't you, Dave?'

Wilson nodded.

'He was going like a bloody train,' he said. 'Then his shot hit the crossbar. I have always took that as some sort of a Sign, narmean? A kind of hush come over the ground, dinnit Kev? It give you the opportunity to expound your wossname, theory. If Simon had put it in the net, I would prob'ly still be down the jobcentre.'

I finished scribbling, and looked up again from my notebook.

'And your theory, based upon this computer print-out, was, quite simply, that Jesus survived the Crucifixion and married a publisher?'

'In a nutshell, yes,' replied Kevin. 'See, I was mucking about with the computer, trying to find out how to make a fortune in publishing, due to where there is not a big future up Telecom Accounts, Catford, in my considered view. When I seen Harold Robbins on the telly lolling on his yacht off Antibes with a couple of large topless numbers rubbing his sun-oil in, I said to myself: he never got *them* by banging off quarterly reminders, domestic. So I punched in all the information I could, and I couldn't believe what come out!'

'The famous theory, eh?' I said, smiling.

'Not at first. At first I got nine thousand Heavy Goods Vehicle licences and a John Lewis Final Demand for £0000000.00, i.e. nothing out of the ordinary up Catford Telecom, but after I'd got Maintenance in to give it a couple of kicks, it suddenly all come spilling out.' He leaned forward, queerly flushed by the recollection. 'It turned out that, following the Crucifixion, far and away the most commercially successful area of publishing was religious books! Up until 33 AD it had been gardening and desk diaries, but since the Resurrection it had been religion, definitely.'

'Really?' I said.

'No question,' said Dave Wilson. 'Soon as Kev told me that, I twigged, din't I? *In the beginning was the Word,* catch my drift?'

'Not entirely,' I admitted.

Dave tutted, and rolled his eyes.

'Jesus survives the cross, right, doubtless due to inferior Roman workmanship or similar. Ask anyone with a Fiat. He lies low for a day or so, probably to stimulate interest in the buying public, before He reappears and gets 'em all going on the Gospels.'

'Good Lord!' I gasped.

'*Smart* Lord!' replied Kevin. 'Getting 'em to do four contradictory accounts was genius, wonnit, Dave?'

'Magic!' replied his colleague. 'It was the foundation of all religious publishing. It set the pattern. It meant that forever afterwards, if you wanted to make a few bob, you came out with a religious book saying the last religious book was a load of cod's wallop. It was like having your own Mint.'

'Fascinating!' I cried. 'And where did Herr Keppel's own remarkable lines of research cross yours?'

'Call it fate,' said Dave. 'Me and Kev had been doing some preliminary investigations into where this computer evidence might lead us, e.g. large villa up Cape Ferret, white Roller out front, all that, when we suddenly had to go to Basel on account of QPR was playing a friendly against Sporting Toblerone. There was a bit of a barney in the crowd due to Tony Currie accidentally killing the Toblerone goalkeeper when he was off the ball, and in the police van we got talking to Heinrich. Turned out he was working in the same field.'

I glanced at the little accountant, and a ballbearing eye stared brightly back.

'You vill,' he said, 'of *Der Verlegerschatz* undoubtedly heard have?'

I nodded. I felt my heart miss a beat.

'The fabled Secret Hoard of the Publishers?' I replied. 'Yes, Herr Keppel, I have. Is it not the legendary source of that impenetrable mystery whereby, whenever an author approaches a publisher, he is told that there is no money for publishing these days and he should count himself lucky his advance is as high as five hundred pounds, but whenever a publisher approaches some fashionable crank who claims that God is an astronaut or Jesus a mushroom, he is able, somehow, to lay his hands on half a million?'

'Exactlich!' cried Keppel. 'Und have you never yourself asked: wherefrom comes this money?'

'Who has not?' I murmured.

Keppel's thin lips twitched, briefly, into a knowing smile.

'I have,' he said, 'incontrovertible evidence that *Der Verlegershatz* in reality a secret numbered account is, into which *every large publisher in the world* huge amounts of money pours, an Emergency Religious Book-Advance Pool to constitute!'

He sat back, in a triumphant beam.

'But where,' I cried, 'do these amounts themselves come from?'

'From the original Mrs Christ Publishing Company, *natürlich!*'

'No!' I shouted.

'Straight up,' said Dave.

'No question,' said Kevin. 'All the various Bible profits down the years, all the Aramaic and Syriac and Greek texts, all the translations, all the hymnal and catechistic spin-offs, all the Latin psalters, authorised versions, revised versions, New English versions, all the prayer-books – have you ever reckoned up the profits, son, never mind percentages on the vestments, chasubles, candles, censers ... I trust I do not need to draw pictures?'

'*And*,' said Dave, banging the matchless Sheraton sofa-table with such force that the deductible Calder mobile above it trembled to a halt and began, slowly, to revolve in the opposite direction, '*and*, we have incontrovertible evidence that this money is channelled into every top publishing house via a member of the executive board who is a direct descendant of the original Christ family! For the past two thousand years, they have been marrying and intermarrying like nobody's business, haven't they, Kev?'

'There's eight of them at Penguin alone,' said his colleague.

'And you claim,' I pressed, 'that you have hard evidence of all this?'

Kevin Betty waved a ring-glittering hand to indicate the Kazakh rugs, the Gobelin tapestries, the six space invaders machines.

'They give us half a million in advance on a bloody synopsis!' he exclaimed scornfully. 'There's no harder evidence than that, sunshine.'

'I hope for all your sakes it will hold water,' I murmured.

'Hold water?' cried Dave. 'It'll bloody walk on it! Until, of course, an entirely new revolutionary and staggering book comes along to refute it and make another few million large ones.'

'Another one?' I said. 'Such as?'

'Such as,' replied Kevin. 'The astonishing *No He Wasn't A Publisher After All, He Was Left-Half For Swansea*, which we understand is coming out next year.'

'Good heavens! Who is doing that one?'

'We are,' said Dave. 'You wouldn't believe the amount of incontrovertible evidence we got left over from our last one.'

I stood up, and closed my notebook.

'Thank you, gentlemen,' I said. 'This has been a truly wonderful experience.'

'Go with God,' said Kevin.

Gardeners' Question Time

CHAIRMAN Good evening, and welcome to the Choams-leigh Village Hall, I'm sure the audience has a veritable host of fascinating questions for our team of experts, so let's go straight into the first question from, I hope I'm pronouncing the name right, Mr John Smith. Is that correct, Mr Smith?

SMITH More or less. In my garden, I have got a Large Danish Au Pair that comes out in sunny weather, usually down by the azaleas, and my question is, how do I stop the bastard next door from attempting to communicate with her through a knot-hole?

CHAIRMAN Thank you, Mr Smith, an interesting one to start us off, perhaps you'd like to take this, Professor Alan Gemmell?

GEMMELL Surely. And I know that the first thing that's occurred to all of us here on the panel is how strange it is to find an example of the Large Danish Au Pair flourishing quite as far west as this.

SMITH Well, she is more of a Mother's Help, really.

GEMMELL Even so, even so. The Large Danish is usually confined to the Greater London area, isn't that right, Bill Sowerbutts?

SOWERBUTTS Almost invariably. They were introduced into this country a few years ago, mostly in Central London, where they did quite well indoors, provided they were left alone and not interfered with. But attempts to relocate them away from their natural habitat of obstetric clinics, discos, falafal houses and so on generally brought disastrous results, did they not, Clay Jones?

JONES They rapidly declined, Bill Sowerbutts. Often,

they would disappear entirely overnight. Tell me, Mr Smith, when you say *Large*, is that a precise definition? Or is she merely big?

SMITH Well, I am not an expert, but she has got thighs like a white mare and you could stand a beer-mug on her bust.

CHAIRMAN Does that answer your query, Clay Jones?

JONES Absolutely. It's obviously a remarkable example, I can see why Mr Smith is worried about something happening to her. What exactly is the threat posed by your neighbour, would you say?

SMITH He mutters things to her, she goes red, and she breaks dinnerware for anything up to two days following. Also, she sometimes shrieks out loud at his remarks and frightens the life out of the cat.

And before you suggest plugging up the knot-hole, I have to tell you that the arris-rails being on his side, the fence is legally his. I have sought professional advice and they say there is sod-all I can do.

SOWERBUTTS I'm afraid they have a point, Mr Smith. It is one of the problems with the Large Danish. All I can suggest is that you try growing something around her, such as a yew-hedge; actually attempting to grow something *on* her, for example one of the denser climbing dog-roses, would probably be a mistake, wouldn't you say, Professor Alan Gemmell?

GEMMELL Definitely. It would have to be a tub-grown to enable her to come indoors and make the beds etcetera, and before you knew it the staircarpet would be full of worms. Perhaps the best course would be to get rid of her altogether and put in a Small Filipino. There is a variety that has a hairy upper lip and flat chest which is fully neighbour-resistant. Also available in couples, to grace any patio.

CHAIRMAN Thank you, team. The next teaser comes from Mr Wilfred Dwyer, who, if I may summarize his rather long question, wants to know what he should do about the swine who has walked off with his pruning hook. Does that put it in a nutshell, Mr Dwyer?

90

DWYER Yes. He borrowed it a fortnight ago to lop his plum, he said, but it transpired that this was a subterfuge, I think the word is. What he used it for was enlarging a knot-hole, which has probably taken the bloody edge off it for a start, but never mind that, we shall cross that bridge when we come to it, my problem is I cannot attract his attention to ask for it back because he is always on the far side of the garden gazing through his fence. I have tried shouting, but it sets the cat off two doors up and I have enough trouble with that madman Smith as it is, he is under the impression that I am up on the roof with my binoculars watching his bloody Swede or whatever she is, when in reality I am merely attempting to locate my pruning hook, I got a willow-tree like a bleeding triffid.

SOWERBUTTS Not an easy one this, is it. Professor Alan Gemmell, what would be the course taken by an expert horticulturalist?

GEMMELL Well, an expert horticulturalist, faced with someone who refused to return a pruning hook, would almost certainly spray him with paraquat. An ordinary garden spray might not reach to the far fence, of course, but then the expert would know exactly where to lay his hands on a commercial high-action spray, or have a friend with a light aircraft prepared to spray from above, choosing a morning when there wasn't much wind about. I find farmers are usually pretty helpful in this, as in most matters where folding money might be involved. What do you think, Clay Jones, a twenty per cent solution?

JONES More than adequate, I should say, Professor Alan Gemmell. It would be enough to induce paralysis and blindness, without actually killing the recipient out-right. This would enable you to nip over the fence while he was writhing about in his agony-throes and ask him where the pruning hook was. However, it should be pointed out that Mr Dwyer is *not* an expert horticultur-alist. For the amateur gardener, it is probably simpler either to chuck a brick at the bastard, or hire a local labourer to go round and break his legs.

CHAIRMAN Yes, we get a lot of letters to the programme about all the heavy work that often has to be done in a garden, and our advice is invariably: *get someone in!* It's usually cheapest in the long run. Next question, please. Mr Nodes?

NODES Thank you. What, in the team's opinion, is the best method of setting fire to a willow tree?

CHAIRMAN Wouldn't it be simpler to chop it down?

NODES No. It would involve hiring a local labourer to go round and break the legs of the man next door first, on account of the tree is in his garden. Or some of it is. Most of it is hanging over my ornamental pond, with the result that blackbird droppings have killed my goldfish, i.e. £14.30 to date. It is what is known as an ecological cycle, I believe: little fly-type objects get attracted to the willow leaves what are hanging over my pond, the goldfish come up to grab the flies, and the blackbirds in the tree crap on their heads.

CHAIRMAN Have you suggested to your neighbour that he prune the tree?

NODES Frequently, but just mentioning the word pruning hook drives him spare, due to where it is currently in the possession of someone who uses it to communicate with a Norwegian next door to him. Anyway, he's on the roof all day with a pair of binoculars, and if I shout about the willow tree so's he can hear me behind the chimney, it sets the cat off three doors up, and I have enough trouble with that madman Smith as it is.

SOWERBUTTS Rather than set fire to it, might it not be better to make a feature of the tree?

NODES You mean cricket bats?

SOWERBUTTS No, no, no. I was thinking of some imaginative scheme whereby the tree could actually be incorporated into your garden. For example, a –

NODES It's a bit bloody late for that, son, what my good lady and I are currently working on is an imaginative scheme for excorporating it from the house, we made the mistake of leaving our bedroom window open last night and next thing I knew I was being woken up at four o'bloody clock this morning by fledglings hopping off the duvet.

CHAIRMAN Well, I'm afraid there doesn't seem to be an immediate answer to this questioner's problem, listeners, but if any of you can come up with something, the address to write to is in the *Radio Times* so can we turn now to Mr Arthur Breene in the hope that we can be a little more successful with him?

BREENE Good evening, team, what in your opinion is the best way of getting dead goldfish off a lawn? It is a curious phenomenon, but they just come flying over the fence and when Mrs Breene or me or her mother Mrs Renee Todd come running out into the garden, there they are dead. Is there such a thing as flying goldfish from e.g. tropical climes and so forth that migrate to our shores and possibly fall exhausted after the long trip and bang their heads on the lawn, causing death? Or could it be that we are the site of something such as the legendary Goldfish's Graveyard, they come up Omdurman Crescent via some strange instinct as old as time itself to snuff it on our premises?

CHAIRMAN What a fascinating question! One, I'm sure, for Professor Alan ...

Oh, Dem Golden Snippers!

It is scant exaggeration to say that when I hobbled into the surgery of Doctor Glaubersaltz for my regular weekly visit on that fateful October morning in 19 –, the shock to the system of one so delicate might well have done for me on the spot. Indeed, I remember thinking, as the giddy turn took its fearful hold: 'This, if I pull through, is good for at least eight more visits, plus untold gallons of the cherry-flavoured miracle drug!'

It was not so much the new flock wallpaper of the waiting-room, nor the shin-deep Uzbekh rugs that now covered the familiar dun lino, as the stunning vision for which these were mere background. Gone was his clog-shod beast of a receptionist, a woman with the figure and the compassion of a Meccano crane, and in her place, lolling against a priceless Sheraton escritoire as she plucked my appointment card from her scarlet garter, stood a Gauguinesque creature of such blood-pounding loveliness that, had Glaubersaltz been not a GP but a cardiologist, I should have accused him of stationing her there solely to drum up business.

'Hi,' she murmured, exposing a row of teeth like enamelled Rennies behind which I caught sight of a

94

coral tongue lurking in the hot depths of her mouth, as if poised to strike, 'Doctor Glaubersaltz will see you *now*!'

I had heard a woman breathe *now* like that only once or twice in my life, and I recalled that on each occasion I had been required to be fully fit: I therefore sidled cautiously past her, and through the door into Glaubersaltz's surgery.

He was wearing a four-hundred-guinea suit, and a broad smile. It was the first time in all my eight-hundred-odd visits that I had ever seen Doctor Glaubersaltz smile. Hitherto, he had habitually looked upon me as some sort of hypochondriac, despite the occasion in May 1972, when I presented with a graze that had needed an entire piece of Elastoplast.

He actually stood up; he held out his hand across the desk; he shook mine.

'Terrific to see you again!' he cried. 'What seems to be the trouble?'

'I think I may have contracted a slight chill,' I replied. 'It may not be much, though.'

Glaubersaltz sprang from his new hide chair, snatched up his stethoscope, his spatulas, his opthalmoscope. I noticed that all were, for some reason, gold-plated.

'May not be *much*?' he exclaimed. 'A slight *chill*? Good God, man, have you any idea where that could lead? Strip, lie down, and, above all, try to be a brave little soldier!'

I lay on his couch; as he probed, and sighed, and tutted, I said:

'You have a new receptionist.'

'You noticed?' he replied, peeling off a rubber glove, not without distaste. 'A wonderful girl, formerly a *chanteuse* at the Kickback Placebo Company sauna in Geneva, you know. I have become a big customer of theirs; they did not stand in her way.' He pursed lips which had been clearly been recently chewed by teeth other than his own. 'Look, call me an old worry-guts if you will, but I would willingly wager my new Lotus that what you have is Collis-Brown's Syndrome.'

A tremor rippled through my supine frame.

'Collis-Brown's Syndrome? Is that bad?'

He shrugged.

'That is not for a humble GP to say. Fortunately, however, I happen to be a close friend and colleague of Dr Collis-Brown himself, medical consultant at St. Moritz's and a household word wherever baccarat is played. Let me ring him.'

I dressed, and Glaubersaltz dialled.

'Nat? Oh, not so bad, another day another dollar, heh-heh-heh! Look, I think I have a new sufferer. I know it makes two gross this week, but can you handle it? Terrific! Personally, I think we can go all the way on this one.' Glaubersaltz smiled modestly into the mouthpiece. 'Don't mention it. Okay, okay, possibly a small TV for the rear seat. I'll send him round.'

Though a tall man, Dr Collis-Brown was dwarfed by the nuclear reactor behind him. He patted it proudly.

'You're looking at seven million pounds, laddie,' he murmured. 'It makes one feel rather humble, does it not?'

'It could,' I said, 'have been no easy task persuading the St Moritz board to purchase it.'

He nodded.

'Metros all round,' he said. 'Not exactly a negligible slice of one's percentage. Still, there is no other treatment for Collis-Brown's Syndrome, so there we are. Progress, laddie, onward and upward, eh?'

He led me into a cubicle, closed the door; after a minute or two, the cubicle was shaken by a reverberant humming, and filled with an indeterminately eerie glow. Some of my skin fell off.

'Some of my skin fell off,' I said to Dr Collis-Brown, when the door re-opened.

'You too?' he replied. He made a note on a scratch-pad, ripped the page out, and threw it in a wastebin. 'Never mind, you have just won yourself a go on Charlene, if you keep your trap shut about the skin. She is a big brunette, with a wide range of mechanical aids.'

I shook my head.

'I don't feel too well just now,' I said.

'Suit yourself. Doubtless you would prefer,' he suddenly whipped a cloth from the table beside him, 'something from the tray, up to a limit of fifty pounds? How about a nice food-mixer? Or perhaps an elegant TV table, chromium legs, smart no-skid casters?'

I chose a pop-up toaster and a set of Jane Austen in elegant tattitex; Dr Collis-Brown made as if to shake my hand, and changed his mind.

'I think I'd like my colleague to have a look at that falling skin,' he said.

I followed a pleasant nude nurse down the long white corridors, and fetched up at last outside a door marked: Albert Nostrum, Consultant Surgeon. I knocked, and went in.

Mr Nostrum was standing at the window, gazing down on a new white Corniche. He turned, eventually.

'We seem to have something of a dilemma here,' he said.

I put down my toaster and my books. My hands peeled.

'Really?' I said, nervously.

'Yes,' he said. 'Personally, I would prefer the numberplate AN 1. The Nippon Surgical Equipment Company, however, are trying to insist on NSE 1.'

'I don't think that was part of the deal,' murmured one of the blondes from the circular bed, 'as I recall.'

'Right!' snapped the surgeon. 'I have already had the hospital purchase two million poundsworth of their damned ironmongery, I do not see why I should drive around advertising their wares like some cheap obstetrics hustler.' He turned back to me, still snarling. 'What's *your* problem?'

'I have a slight chill,' I said, 'and my skin is falling off.'

He nodded.

'Surgery,' he said, 'is the only answer. Fortunately, I have this fantastic new range of Jap hardware, just in. See this? This is a laser saw, that's what this is!'

'What does it cut off?' I enquired faintly.

'What *doesn't* it cut off!' cried Nostrum. 'These slants may try to bilk you on the small print, but when it comes to slicing, there is no-one within a mile of 'em! I can do anything with this, heads included. What do you want lopped?'

'Isn't that,' I shut my eyes, 'rather up to you?'

'I don't see that,' he replied. 'Are you after the box of Havanas, the folding bike, or the holiday-of-a-lifetime for two on the famed Belgian Riviera?'

'What do you suggest?' I murmured.

'Personally,' replied the surgeon. 'I would go for the big one. It would help me justify buying all this kit if I could snip out a lung or two. If you opted for the holiday, I would be prepared to kick in some nice luggage, at my personal expense.'

I sat down, and allowed the room to settle around me.

'I think,' I said, 'that I should like a second opinion.'

He looked at me, with sudden respect.

'I underestimated you,' he said. 'That is a very wise decision indeed. With a second opinion, you get a canteen of cutlery. It so happens my esteemed colleague Lionel Charlatan FRCS has just closed a truly fantastic deal with a major international transplant bank.' Mr Nostrum pressed an intercom button. 'Bosie,' he murmured, 'would you ask your boss to step in here a minute?'

It was six long months before I had recovered sufficiently to be ambulanced back to Doctor Glaubersaltz's surgery for my post-operative check-up. He had, by this time, moved from Willesden to Harley Street. His door was opened by several members of the Young Generation in lizard-skin waders, who showed me up to the doctor's penthouse suite.

'Long time, no see,' said Doctor Glaubersaltz. 'I hardly recognized you under that plastic surgery.'

'My skin fell off,' I explained, through new lips.

'These slight chills can be nasty,' said Glaubersaltz.

'I have one lung,' I said, 'and a Korean kidney.'

'Interesting,' he murmured. 'And tell me – how's the chill?'

'It seems to have gone,' I said.

Glaubersaltz beamed.

'What did I tell you?' he cried. 'There's nothing that medicine can't do, these days.'

For Their Cars Only

'Yes, I find everything about James Bond believable, except in one respect. The girls, the fights, the villains, the plots, they're all exactly like my own domestic life. How come our cars are so different?'

Alan Coren, in an interview with Kenneth Harris

A scant furlong ahead of Bond's hurtling Bentley, the Type 59 Bugatti slewed through the rain-slicked roundabout and took off down the long Basingstoke straight like an Oerlikon shell, the whine of its Scintilla-Vertex magneto hurling the terrified pheasants from the shaking hedgerows.

Selecting, as he twitched out of the bend, a plumpish brace, Bond dropped them with successive shots from his 9mm Walther PPK, and smiled. He would be back to collect them soon enough: the Bugatti was at its limit, the Bentley had a clear ten miles per hour edge, the jig was inescapably up. He cut in the Siemens AF4 supercharger, and began to close on Goldfinger.

It was at that instant that his race-tuned ears picked up the tink-tink-tink from somewhere deep inside the pedigree bowels. It became a tonk-tonk-tonk. Something else went fneu-fneu-fneu. The twenty layers of Bicker-mole & Whymper cellulose on the Hooper bonnet began to deckle. The car lost speed.

Bond, with no other choice, flung the Bentley off the road into a fortuitous Mobil forecourt, cursed, sprang out, threw up the bonnet.

A small overalled man appeared beside him.

'You know what that is, don't you?' said the mechanic.

100

'What?' cried Bond, relieved.

'Smoke,' said the mechanic. 'You see a lot of that in my job. You get to recognize it.'

Bond glared into the drizzled distance. Goldfinger's Bugatti was a dwindling dot.

'How long would it take to fix it?' he said.

The mechanic looked at his watch.

'Twelve days,' he said. 'Give or take. I'm on the pumps till Thursday week, due to Norman being in Doncaster with his Auntie May's thrombosis.'

'For God's sake, this is an emergency!' shouted Bond. 'Can't you leave the damn pumps, surely there's –'

'*Leave* the pumps?' cried the mechanic, reeling. 'You cannot *leave* pumps, son! You got to watch 'em every minute. They're like children, pumps.'

Bond looked at him for some time, through slitted eyes. The man sniffed. In the driving rain, Bond's lightweight Collinson & Breene trousers began to shrink slowly up his shins.

'Very well,' he gritted, at last. 'May I use your phone?'

'The appliance,' said the mechanic, indicating a hand-lettered sign, 'is for the use of bona fide customers only. We are not a public wossname.'

Bond ripped open his Jellinek & Sampson peccadillo-hide wallet, and thrust a ten-pound note into the man's hand.

'Petrol,' he said hoarsely.

The mechanic looked at the note.

'This qualifies you,' he said, 'either for a Free Sherry Glass voucher or a Viscount Linley spring-loaded tea-towel hook. Which do you want?'

'Oh God,' said Bond, and hit the mechanic behind the ear with a deft Kyoto chop.

Then he dialled the AA.

The rain had lifted when, some two hours later, the AA arrived. The mechanic was still sleeping gently beside his pump. Bond was eating Valium. Goldfinger would be pulling into Parliament Square by now.

'Was you the gentleman,' said the AA man, opening his snaplock briefcase and unscrewing the monogrammed Sheaffer with which a grateful Association had rewarded his ten thousandth sale of *Reader's Digest* socket sets, 'who wanted the *Pop-Up Book of British Mice*, or was you the party wishing to take advantage of our combined Room Extension Insurance and Two Hang-Gliding Holidays For The Price Of One Offer?'

Bond examined a manicured nail.

'No,' he murmured, 'no, I'm the party who shoots people.'

The AA van drove fairly well, all in all, despite the weight of stuffed animals, folding picnic tables, Black Forest simulated-teak barometers, desk-sets, feeler-gauges, cufflinks, Rubik-cube keyrings, and boxed sets of the *Encyclopaedia Digestiana*. It was not, of course, the Bentley, but he made reasonable time until he reached Sunbury, at which point several hundred cuckoo clocks, reduced for clearance, began a low muffled cackling from the piled containers behind his head. Bond glanced quickly at his Patek-Phillipe.

It was noon.

Four hours to Goldfinger's drear deadline.

Bond reached for his cigarette-case, flicked it open: it was empty. He pulled the AA van into the kerb, leapt out, jinked desperately between the thronging shoppers, and ran into a tobacconist's. There being a slight delay due to Bond's inability to translate into passable Gujarati his request for a packet of Hagermann & Snipstone's Perfectos Finos Number 33, it was almost five minutes before, resignedly clutching a carton of Silk Cut and (for some reason he could not begin to comprehend) a quarter of Dolly Mixtures, he regained the van.

It now had GLEN HODLE SNIFS aerosoled down one flank, and BLACKS GO HOAM down the other.

Its wheels were gone.

Bond stared at it, rocking slightly on his elegant heels.

'I blame the parents,' said a passing vicar.

*

'Avis Davis here,' murmured the mellifluous voice at the other end of the phone, 'your pleasure is our duty.'

'I need,' shouted James Bond, startled by the unprofessional wildness in the eyes that stared wretchedly back at him from the phone booth's remaining sliver of mirror, 'I *urgently* need an extremely fast car –'

'From our astoundingly extensive range of Jaguars, Mercedes, BMWs, or other fine executive high-performance, yet competitively priced, automobiles sir?' thrummed the girl.

'Exactly!' cried Bond. 'Can you deliver it to the Sunbury Odeon in the next thirty minutes and charge it to my account?'

'Consider it done, sir,' replied the girl. 'Do you have any particular preference as to colour, upholstery trim, make of stereo, or –'

'No, no, no!' snapped Bond. 'Any Mercedes or Jag, that'll be fine, quick as you like!'

It was hardly more than three hours later when the Fiat 127 rattled up.

'See, I had it down as *Sudbury*,' said the delivery driver, 'know what I mean? Basically, it is on account of them silly mares on the fourth floor not pressing hard enough on the chit. You got to really *press*, know what I mean, or it don't come through on the bottom copy, are you with me? So –'

'Why is it a Fiat 127?' said Bond, very quietly.

The man looked at him, puzzled.

'It is *always* a Fiat 127,' he said.

'I ordered a Mercedes,' said Bond, 'or, failing that, a –'

'Course you did,' said the driver. 'Now, there's just one thing you got to watch on this one, it's got a funny tendency to wander all over the road, also I wouldn't drive it in rain, water gets in through them little vents and shorts out the distributor, but you're all right so long as it's dry. Not dry and *hot*, mind, on account of it's got a funny tendency to overheat when it's hot, and whatever you do, don't try winding the window down, I got a bit of fag-packet holding it just right.'

103

'Oh good,' said Bond.

'I wouldn't slam the door,' said the man, handing Bond his clipboard for sixteen signatures, 'that exhaust's only held on with Sellotape.'

Despite the Avis Davis strictures, Bond had managed to wind the Fiat up to nearly sixty mph on the Chiswick Flyover, this being just a little less than the speed at which the white Rover overtook him, and waved him into the kerb.

Bond stopped, and tried to wind the window down. The piece of cardboard having been duly dislodged, the window fell on the sergeant's foot.

'Oh dearie me,' said the sergeant. 'It would not appear to be our day, sir.'

'Is this your exhaust-pipe sir?' enquired the constable, having retrieved it from the distant spot at which Bond had first attempted to brake. He passed it through the glassless window, onto Bond's lap.

'My name is James Bond,' said the agent. He flipped open his department billfold. 'And this is my authority.'

The sergeant looked at the green plastic rectangle.

'Goodness me, Dennis,' he said to the constable, 'this gentleman has been to Disneyland.'

The constable craned.

'Cobblers,' he said, 'you can get them up Hamley's. They come with a packet of false conks and a magnifying wossname.'

'I take it that is your own nose, sir,' said the sergeant, peering so closely that the faint aroma of salt-and-vinegar from his moustache mingled strangely with the Monsieur Rochas wafting off Bond's polished chin.

Bond did not flinch.

'Tell me,' he said, 'have you seen a Type 59 Bugatti on this road at any time during the past few hours?'

'Bugatti?' repeated the sergeant. 'Do we know anything about any Bugatti, Dennis?'

The constable kicked the Fiat's bald tyre. It sighed, and flattened.

'Very nice, Bugatti,' he said. 'Grate a bit of that artisan cheese on top, it goes down a treat.'

Bond tensed his muscles against the inevitable denouement. But first he said, very carefully:

'It is being driven by the most dangerously maniacal criminal upon this planet. In the boot, he has secreted a thermonuclear device capable of wiping out the whole of Greater London. He will trigger this device in exactly –' he flicked a cold glance at his watch '– eighteen minutes and forty-two seconds, unless I can get to him first.'

The constable looked at the sergeant. The sergeant looked at James Bond. He opened the Fiat's door.

'I think we might start, sir,' he said, 'by having a look at the steering.'

Bond, the door gaping, sprang.

Unfortunately, however, the long day's weary doings had taken, all unnoticed, their heavy toll. Bond was a fraction slower than he might otherwise have been, and the young constable, having all along suspected from the combination of battered old car and public school accent that Bond might be a dangerous Trotskyite sociologist of some kind, was poised for instant action.

The truncheon thwacked down upon Bond's well-groomed head, and he fell senseless to the tarmac.

Beneath the flyover, Greater London stretched away towards the smogged horizon, huge, human, vulnerable. The precious seconds ticked slowly and inexorably by.

Not, of course, that it mattered. Goldfinger having, some two hours before, parked on a double yellow line in order to nip into Praed Street gents, the Bugatti had immediately been towed away.

A Little Parky

The chat show has become more than mere entertain-ment: it is now a part of the culture, not only informing how we act and speak but actually setting out new patterns for social behaviour. – New Society

A suburban drawing-room, evening. From the Nattitrak ceiling fixture, six spotlights beat pitilessly down upon a circle of four tubular chromium chairs drawn up around a low glass table bearing four tumblers and a water-jug. In one of the chairs sits Kevin Bracewell, legs crossed, a clipboard on his knee. From time to time, he grins to himself, chortles, raises eyebrows in turn, tugs at his pepper-and-salt hairpiece, plucks invisible lint from his blue serge knee, glances up, beaming, at the corners of the room. The door opens. He leaps up, and bounds across, hands outstretched, to meet his first guest. It is his wife, Sharon, hobbling awkwardly in a new sequinned sheath, her tourmaline hair winking in the fierce wattage. She smiles an enormous smile, dislodging from her left cheek a beauty spot which floats down and settles on her cleavage. Kevin clasps her hand in both of his, she kisses him on the cheek (leaving a magenta ring), he leads her to a chair, she catches her heel and stumbles. At this, they both laugh immoderately, heads thrown back, for some time.

KEVIN It's always doing that, ha-ha-ha!
SHARON Ha-ha-ha! Is it?
KEVIN Yes! Ha-ha-ha!
SHARON Ha-ha-ha!

KEVIN Oh, dear! (*wipes his eye*) No, but seriously, it's great to have you back here again, Sharon, it really truly is.

SHARON Well, it's wonderful to *be* back here, Kevin!

KEVIN I must say, it seems like ages. It must be, what –?

SHARON Two hours.

KEVIN *Two hours?*

SHARON Two hours!

KEVIN I should think a lot's happened to you since then, Sharon. Tell me, what have you been doing?

SHARON I've been kicking the dishwasher, Kevin.

KEVIN What?

SHARON Ha-ha-ha, you look surprised, Kevin. I think I've surprised Kevin, everyone! I think I've shaken that famous composure, haven't I, Kevin?

KEVIN Well, ha-ha-ha, I am a little surprised, Sharon. Tell me, this dishwasher-kicking, is it a new venture for you?

SHARON In a way I suppose it is, Kevin, yes. Of course, in a career like mine –

KEVIN A highly successful career, might I say, Sharon?

SHARON Thank you, Kevin, but there is naturally a side to it that the public never sees, a lonely, private side, Kevin, when a person looks at herself and says *Where am I going?*, do you know that feeling, Kevin?

KEVIN Well, speaking personally, Sharon, I have never been a successful wife and mother with a detached house in matured grounds of nearly half an acre with my own midnight-blue Austin Metro and an account at John Lewis, ha-ha-ha, so I'm not sure I can actually put myself in your, tell me more about this new dishwasher-kicking avenue that has opened up, won't you, Sharon?

SHARON It's not terribly new, Kevin, it sort of naturally followed on from some of my recent experiments with throwing the toaster through the window and banging my head on the wall of the bathroom.

KEVIN On the wall of one of your *two* bathrooms, wouldn't I be right in saying, Sharon?

SHARON Yes, that's correct, Kevin.

KEVIN Just so that no-one gets the wrong impression, Sharon, ha-ha-ha! But, surely, your career is going wonderfully just now, isn't it? Didn't I read somewhere that you have a new rota coming out?

SHARON Yes, that's so, Kevin, I should think you probably saw that on the kitchen blackboard.

KEVIN As I understand it, this will be your fourth school rota in as many years, that's quite a record! And this time won't you be working with (*he glances down at his clipboard*) Tracy Foskett, Miranda Cleghan, and that fabulous newcomer, Debbie Wickfield? Sounds more like fun than work, Sharon!

SHARON Does it, Kevin? Well, I suppose to the general public it might, but they of course don't see all the painstaking effort and organization that goes into the making of a major modern school rota, do they, Kevin? They do not realize, for example, that I have to be dressed and in full make-up before it gets light, and then, of course, there is the perennial problem, in my profession, of working with children.

KEVIN I always thought you liked children, Sharon, ha-ha-ha!

SHARON Ha-ha-ha! I cannot stand the little swine, Kevin!

KEVIN Well, that's really fascinating, Sharon, I'm sure that's come as a huge surprise to, er, tell me, you've been doing rather a lot of travelling recently, haven't you?

SHARON I'm afraid it goes with the job, Kevin, although I know that to people outside the profession it looks like one long round of fun, rushing to glamorous places like Bejam and Sainsbury's, suddenly finding yourself in completely unfamiliar car parks, meeting new people who've mistakenly slipped in front of you at the check-out or driven into your offside front wing or – by the way, Kevin, and forgive me, it *is* your show, *I* shouldn't be asking the questions, ha-ha-ha, but what made you refer to newcomer Debbie Wickfield as fabulous?

KEVIN Ha-ha-ha, Sharon (*wrinkles his eyes, simpers,*

fiddles with his clipboard, looks up at the lights, picks his nose, grins boyishly, scratches his hairpiece with his pencil), that's really one from left field, as we say on Broadway, but by 'eck, as my old Dad used to say, she is a reet bobby dazzler, bai goom, and he knew a thing or two, did my old Dad, 'e wur nobbut so griddle as wick! Did you know he played cricket for Blackburn, Sharon?

SHARON   Tell me about Debbie, Kevin.

KEVIN   Well, Sharon, we'll be meeting her later on, along with another fabulous guest, but tell me, with all this tearing about the countryside, I suppose that doesn't leave much time for romance?

SHARON   I'm afraid it doesn't, Kevin, and one's career does rather take it out of one, you know, my name has not been romantically linked with anyone for six months, ha-ha-ha!

KEVIN   (*consults clipboard*) Ten, actually, ha-ha-ha!

SHARON   Is it really? My, doesn't time fly when you're having fun, Kevin, ha-ha-ha!

KEVIN   Ha-ha-ha! Well, Sharon, that's more or less brought us up to date, I know you're going to want to tell me about your fabulous future plans, but before we get around to that, and I think I hear them at the door now (*he springs up, runs his tongue over his teeth, grins, straightens his tie, smooths his hairpiece, shoots his cuffs, runs out, calls, invisible, from the hall*) – will you give a very warm and very special welcome to – (*he reappears in the doorway*) – Debbie and Norman Wickfield!

A tall svelte girl in rhinestoned dreadlocks and a lamé chainmail shift shimmers into the room, accompanied by a thick-set bearded man in a brown tweed suit. Their hands are pumped by their beaming host, who settles them in the two remaining chairs.

KEVIN   Debbie and Norman, wonderful to see you, welcome, welcome, welcome! I know it's your first time on, but I know you're not going to be nervous, and Debbie, I think you already know Sharon, don't you?

DEBBIE   Yes, Kevin, we are appearing in a wonderful

new rota together, and I want to say that it has been a wonderful experience working alongside a real old trouper like Sharon who is a really wonderful person, underneath.

KEVIN That's wonderful, Debbie. Tell me, are all the rumours true about your having the longest legs in West Ruislip, ha-ha-ha?

DEBBIE Ha-ha-ha, Kevin, I wouldn't know, *you* tell me! (*She leans forward and squeezes his knee, he laughs and squeezes her thigh, she laughs and squeezes his cheek, he laughs and squeezes her arm.*) No, but seriously, Kevin, do you think my bust is too big? It can be a terrible handicap having long legs and a big bust, people on the rota often do not take your driving seriously.

KEVIN Handicap, ha-ha-ha? Well, speaking for myself, Debbie, I –

NORMAN Good evening, Kevin.

KEVIN Whoops, ha-ha-ha, forgive me, Norman! Good evening, Norman. Norman, before I get back to the lovely Debbie, I know that everyone would like to know what you do. What exactly is it, Norman?

NORMAN I punch people in the mouth, Kevin.

There is a brief scuffle, during which Norman lays out Kevin, and Sharon throws Debbie through the picture window. After a moment or two, Norman and Sharon resume their seats.

NORMAN Good evening, Sharon, it's wonderful to have you here, and I know that the first question everyone will want me to ask is: Is it really true that you intend to go solo at last?

SHARON Well, Norman, obviously I've given the whole matter a great deal of . . .

From the
Alternative Version

And the Lord God took the man and put him into the garden of Eden, to dress it and to keep it. – Genesis 2:15

3 And behold, it was *Spring*, and time for the sod to be turned; and the man went *into* the garden, saying: where is the fork *that* I left over there by the shrubbery, nice and ready, last *Winter*? Wherefore comes it that ye cannot put anything down in a garden for five minutes without someone coming along and nicking it?

2 And the LORD God spake, saying: art thou talking to me?

3 And Adam replied *thusly*, saying: hast thou borrowed my fork?

4 And behold, the LORD God waxed exceeding wrath, and *spoke* to the man in this wise: I am the LORD thy God, and if I want a fork I do not have to nick it. The fork *that* thou leftest by the shrubbery hath through thine own indolence rotted away.

5 But the man replied, saying: why didst thou invent rotting? That was a perfectly good fork. I find thy *ways* exceeding strange, O LORD; thou has put me in this garden to dress it and to keep it, but how am I *to* do this when thou rottest my *implements*? And while we are on the subject, was it thou who has covered the *lawn* in little brown lumps, that it is an eyesore, never mind a billiard table?

6 And the LORD God replied unto Adam, saying: those are *worm droppings*.

7 Whereupon Adam grew exceeding bitter, crying: O LORD who (I assume) maketh the worm, would it *have* interfered mightily with thine eternal plan to have arranged it *so that* it emptied its bowels underground?

8 But the LORD God made no reply, so the man went his *way* to seek out the dahlia tubers which he had raised the previous *Autumn*, that the frost should not get them.

9 And lo, the frost had got them.

10 But the man did not supplicate the LORD to enquire the place of frost in the divine *scheme*, for he knew *that* he should receive some answer that would *make* no sense to him. Likewise did he not bring up the subject of leaf-curl, mildew, rust, black spot, *pear midge*, cutworms, *moss*, thrips, groundsel, root maggot, *shoot flop*, woolly aphis, or wireworms. Instead, fashioned he a new fork for himself, that he might turn the sod for *Spring* planting, the while casting his *eyes* away from the daffodil bulbs where they lay, *lest* he wonder how they had crept out of the earth to lie all over the place, shrivel-ling, and cry out incontinently and incur *the* wrath of the LORD.

11 But lo, when he came to dig the ground with the new fork that he had made, found he not fresh warm earth *as* he had expected; but many small pieces of blue and white saucers.

12 And Adam could keep silent no longer, crying: if I am *the* first to be set here in this place where I am, wherefore cometh it that there are all these broken bloody saucers? Or am I to assume, O LORD, that they were knocked up by the beasts of the field, *for example* a smart rabbit?

13 And the LORD God replied unto Adam, saying: look, the eternal mystery of how it is *that* there are always broken pieces of blue and white saucers wheresoever ye dig is the biggest eternal mystery there is. It is so big, *that* even I do not understand it. That is how big it is.

14 So the man toiled all of that day; and when he had *turned* the sod and removed all the fragments therefrom, put he up a *trellis* on the back wall,

that climbing roses might grow upon it, in their fashion. And in the evening he rested, and the trellis fell on him.

4 Now the LORD God took pity on the man where he lay, saying: *It is* not good that the man should be alone; I will make an help meet for him.

2 And the LORD caused a deep sleep to fall upon Adam, and he slept; and he took one of his ribs, and closed up the flesh instead thereof.

3 And the rib, which the LORD God had taken from the man, made he a woman, and brought her *unto* the man. And the woman looked upon the man and spake, saying: typical, sleeping.

4 And the man stared at her exceeding *hard*, saying: look, I have got this rib-ache, it must be the sudden digging, ye have got *to* take these things slowly, I have not touched a fork all *Winter*, or it could be the weather, I have never known a March like it, it *goes* right through ye, what are those nasty lumps on thy chest?

5 But the woman said, never mind all that, this garden *doth* not look as though it hath had a fork on it *ever*; I do not pretend to be an expert, having been around only six minutes, but women have a sort of an instinct for these things; we are exceeding creative.

6 Whereat Adam answered her in this wise, saying: what dost thou mean *we*, there is only one of ye, and anyway, if there were two it would be womans. One tree, two trees, one God, two, er. What kind of a word is women?

7 And the woman said, typical, arguing. Arguing will not give us a lawn we shall be proud to own, that it shall be an envy of all our neighbours, broad stripes, no couch-grass or clover, provided instructions are carried out as specified.

8 But the man said: what meaneth thou, proud *to* own? What meaneth thou, envy, when there is nobody else to see it, unless of course thou hast a few beasts of the field dropping in for tea, ha ha?

9 And there came upon them in that place where

they stood, thunder; and in the thunder, the voice of the Lord God, saying: wherefore cometh this talk of pride and envy, O woman? Hast thou dared to eat of the fruit *that* I have forbidden unto thee? 10 But the woman replied, saying: eat of what fruit? Pull this one, O Lord, it hath bells on; owing to lack of proper pruning, greased paper encircling trunk, regular spraying, and similar things in this wise too numerous to mention, there is no fruit, forbidden or anything else. It is time that this man was taken in hand.

11 And Adam lifted his eyes *up* to the heavens, crying: O Lord, can I have my rib back? True, it was not a help meet for me, but then it did not give me all this lip, either.

12 But the Lord God replied not.

13 And the woman stood apart awhile in that place where she was, thinking: and at length, she spake unto Adam, saying: I have put my finger on it. What this garden needeth is a pond, to be a *feature* and a conversation piece, also an artificial waterfall for there is nothing like the sound of running water in a garden.

14 But the man fell upon the ground, crying: who needeth a conversation piece? There is only thou and I in this place where we are, and I do not wish to talk about ponds. And indeed, thou art right when thou sayest that there is nothing like the sound of running water in a garden, I hear it often and it invariably meaneth bloody trouble, for example root-rot, subsidence, moss gnats, need I go on? 15 And the woman replied, saying: no. Just dig. 16 Whereupon Adam, seeking only that his life *be* quiet, dug all that day and all that night, even unto darkness *upon* the next day; and when he had finished, he called out to the woman, that she come and admire that pond which he had made.

17 And the woman looked *at the* pond and spake, saying: not there. Over there, by the tree.

5 Thus it was that the man toiled all that *Spring*, even

into *Summer*, digging many beds and making many features *as* the woman indicated unto him. And where there were not beds, were there paths.

2 And where there were not paths, were there rockeries.

3 And where there were not rockeries, were there arbors.

4 And where there were not arbors, were there pergolas.

5 And where there were not pergolas, were there sundials, and penguins, and herons, and large toads; and midgets with big heads holding fishing rods over the many, many ponds. And all of these things were wrought by the man from stone, crying out in great lamentation the whiles; but the LORD God heard him not, in his woe.

6 And thus it came to pass that Adam and his wife were walking in the garden in the cool of the day, that the wife might the better work out the most fit place to set the garden furniture that it might provide the best view of the carriage lamps, the birdbath, the rustic gate, the dovecote and the gazebo that the man had wrought, when they heard the voice of the LORD God.

7 And the LORD God called unto Adam, and said unto him, Where art thou?

8 And Adam said, I heard thy voice in the garden, and I was afraid, because I thought thou might not like the patio that I have made.

9 And the LORD God waxed more wrath than he had hitherto waxed, ever, crying: thou hast taken the garden wherein I set thee and made of it an *eyesore*. Wast thou not satisfied with that which I had vouchsafed *unto* thee? Thou art not fit to dress and keep a window-box, never mind anything else.

10 And Adam cried out in his woe, saying: where wast thou up till now, O LORD? Why didst thou not say anything to me upon this subject earlier?

11 And the LORD God spake unto the man, saying: I was up Alpha Centauri, dividing the waters which were under the firmament from the waters which were above

the firmament. I cannot be everywhere at once. I thought I could trust thee not to *make* a pig's ear of Eden while that I was away; I see that I was wrong.

12 Therefore the Lord God sent him forth from the garden of Eden.

13 So he drove out the man; and he placed at the east of the garden of Eden Cherubims, and a flaming sword which turned every way, to show what really bad taste can do, if ye have the money.

Scheming Spires

News last week that the two children of a Hong Kong businessman were to be admitted to Wadham College, Oxford, with minimum A-level grades in gratitude for a gift of £500,000 came shortly after St. Hugh's College announced a £400,000 gift to its building fund from a Hong Kong group. – The Observer

The warden of Yumyum Freezedried Shrimp College gazed out smugly from his mediaeval mullions across the flawless Astroturf of the Yamaha Quad towards the Durex Library, and found the prospect good.

'Full many a glorious morning have I seen,' he murmured, 'flatter the mountain tops with sovereign eye, kissing with golden face the meadows green, gilding pale streams with heavenly alchemy.'

'Could piss down later, though,' said the Foskett Loft Conversions Professor of European History, 'narmean? Lot of them humorous clouds about.'

'Cumulus,' said the Warden.

'*And* them,' said Professor Foskett, nodding. 'You get to know a bit about mornings in my business. Forty skilled conversion operatives up on the roofs banging in anodized aluminium dormers, sun winking off of the Foskett No-Fuss Childprufe catches, and suddenly it's coming down like a bleeding mongoose, am I right?'

'Monsoon, quite,' murmured the Warden. 'I imagine that that could be most unsettling. *Naturam expellas furca, tamen usque recurrat*, eh?'

'Definitely. You got to get the polythene across like a whippet.' He tapped the Warden on the chest. 'That is

117

what separates the men from the boys in the loft conversion business, son. I did not get where I am today by standing around with my hands in my wossnames watching shrinkage to clients' Axminster, also make good skirting warp, did I?'

The Warden took a reflective sip of the '66 Krug, cheered by both it and the thought that a hundred cases like it now lay beneath him in the college cellars, courtesy of a grateful Yumyum management. Changing the name had been a negligible price to pay. Indeed, Yumyum rather grew on one, he found: it rolled pleasantly off the tongue, particularly if that tongue had been agreeably pre-lubricated. The old rival, Balliol, he recollected happily, had fared far worse in the great sponsorship tussle; it could not be easy to wear the Mastership of Exlax with dignity.

'And now that you *are* where you are today, Professor,' he said, 'are you happy?'

'As a pig in, er!' cried the Professor of European History. 'Not only have I bunged you a new wing, thereby immortalizing Foskett Loft Conversions, especially with the name painted on the roof being visible in Business Class from twenty thousand feet, I have also got four inches in *Who's Who* listing wide range of roof novelties, *plus* captive audience of impressionable young minds every Monday and Thursday, many of them influential wogs from developing countries seeking to lash out a bob or two on smart roofing for the presidential palace, catch my drift?'

The Warden of Yumyum smiled absently, watching a crocodile of pornographers' sons carrying Canalettos towards the Great Hall from their fathers' Bentleys.

'The lectures are going well, then?' he murmured.

'Definitely! Yesterday, we done *The Edict of Nantes With Special Reference To Loft Conversions*, this Thursday I'm giving 'em *Tiling Problems of the Treaty of Utrecht.*'

'And the undergraduates are responding well?' enquired the Warden.

'Hard to say, given that only about four of 'em speak English, but I reckon the message is getting through: when I go up the dais of a morning, they all shout FOSKETT'S FOR LOFTS AND ROOFS!, so you could say I was making progress.'

'Really?'

'No question. First three weeks of term it was FOSKETT'S FOR ROFTS AND LOOFS. Funny thing, your Nip is dead nimble when it comes to bunging them sicilian chips together, but ask 'em to get their tongue round sunnink simple, they bloody near throttle theirselves! I mentioned it to the Kennomeat Professor of Linguistics up the Rat and Cockle yesterday, and it was his professional opinion it was all down to them putting things in the water up Japan.'

'Remarkable,' said the Warden, pouring himself a third glass.

'Yes, they done it in the war to stop 'em surrendering,' said the Professor of European History, 'and it is probably still in the pipes. I heard that from my colleague in the 24-Hour Drains Unblocked No Job Too Large Or Small Oriental History Department. That is one of the great things about Oxford, son, as I am sure I do not have to tell you, the cross-fertilization of specialists. You'd be surprised the tips you can pick up.'

The Warden was about to shape his reply to this, when there was a sharp rap at the door, and he opened it to admit a small man in high-heeled boots; these he now clicked together, hurling the monocle from his left eye. His right arm shot up at an angle of forty-five degrees.

'Yes, Dean?' said the Warden.

'*Entschuldigung, mein Führer!*' shrieked the Dean. 'But last night have I a little yellow degenerate apprehended, who a chamberpot on the top of the Martyrs Memorial just placed had! Can I gas him?'

'No, Dean,' said the Warden. 'Send him to me.'

The Dean ground his teeth, clicked his heels again, saluted, and went out.

'Funny bugger, the Dean,' said the Professor of

119

European History. 'Why won't he tell anybody his name?'

'He was instrumental,' murmured the Warden, 'in retrieving some rather fetching Renoirs for the Warden's Lodging from the bottom of, as I recall, Lake Geneva. In return, I guaranteed him anonymity.'

'He's a troublemaker,' said the Professor. 'Last Tuesday he winged the Sam Rappaport Blouses Lecturer in Applied Mathematics, and a Mossad exchange student bunged a stun grenade through his window. Could've ruined the roof, I speak as one who knows.'

The Warden smiled.

'A great university,' he said gently, 'thrives on controversy.'

He opened the door to a second knock, and a small Malaysian came into the room, and bowed.

'The Dean informs me,' said the Warden, 'that last night you placed a chamberpot on one of Oxford's most respected monuments?'

The undergraduate bowed again.

The Warden reached beneath his gown, and, taking thence a wad of used notes, peeled off a handful of tens. The undergraduate bowed a third time, and left.

'Hallo,' said the Professor of European History.

'We have the Mothercare franchise,' explained the Warden. He drained his fourth glass, slipped his arm beneath his colleague's, and led him towards the door. 'Come, Professor Foskett,' he said, 'today is an important day! Today, we have Torpids.'

'If they're them little pancake efforts with grasshoppers in,' said Professor Foskett, paling, 'you can count me out. All this Yumyum stuff up High Table goes through me like nobody's business.'

'Torpids,' said the Warden, savouring, as they descended the staircase, the luxurious parental gift of the 243 Viceroy Curzon Road Hyderabad Carpet Emporium Scholar, 'are the inter-college boat races. They begin this morning, and I have high hopes of Yumyum!'

They emerged into the balmy morning. The Professor

120

of European History sniffed the heady air.

'Rain's kept off,' he said. He paused. 'That poem of yours,' he said, 'who done it?'

'Shakespeare.'

'Big seller, is he?' enquired the Professor.

'Oh, millions,' replied the Warden. 'Why?'

'I was just wondering whether he couldn't be persuaded to change the first line to *Full many a loft conversion have I seen*,' said the Professor. 'It could open up a whole new wossname.'

'He's dead,' said the Warden.

'No problem, then,' said the Professor. He looked at the Warden, hard. 'It'd be worth a squash court,' he said.

The Warden paused, in the shadow of the College porch.

'I suppose,' he murmured, 'now that the Oxford University Press is the Hokikoki Electronics Publishing Company, they might accept my authority on this interesting textual crux, if you could perhaps...'

'I'll bung 'em a grand,' nodded the Professor. 'No problem.'

So, arms linked, they strode out of Yumyum, crossed Volkswagenstrasse, turned left down Wimpy Street, negotiated a noisy *suttee* outside Trinity & Hedges College, and, despite becoming caught up in a violent demonstration by young Walloon millionaires incensed by the election to the Union presidency of a Flemish-speaking octogenarian property tycoon, arrived in good time at the crowded banks of the twinkling Volvo.

'Capital!' cried the Warden of Yumyum, towering above the polyglot iridescence of the teeming student body loyally waving their company logos, 'the first race is about to start!' Far off, beyond the bend, an unseen cannon cracked. 'ROW UP, YUMYUM!' screamed the Warden.

The boats lurched into view around the bend. The crowd seethed. The Warden craned.

'*Yumyum is leading*!' he bellowed.

The Professor of European History peered upstream.

' 'Ere,' he said. 'There's more than eight blokes in that!'

'Thirty-one, actually,' said the Warden. 'It was a point upon which a number of fathers were somewhat insistent. I see no reason why rules should not be sympathetically interpreted, Professor. A great university must accommodate to changing times. In our last rugger match against Big Mac College, they fielded seventy-three prop forwards, all of whom complained that the ball was oval. Oh, well *rowed*, Yumyum!'

'They've hit the bank!' cried the Professor. 'They're going down like bleeding stones!'

'Aren't they, though?' said the Warden. 'I say, you haven't got a calculator on you, by any chance?'

The Professor shook his head.

'Can they swim?' he muttered, grasping the Warden's sleeve.

'I shouldn't think so for a moment,' replied the Warden. 'Industrial pollution has long persuaded the oriental to natatory circumspection. And even if they could, the following boats would mow... oh my goodness, did you see that? The Mitsubishi boat has speared little Murg Masallah like a spitted quail! *Apparent rari nantes in gurgite vasto*, eh? I say, Professor, do you suppose his father is good for a memorial chapel?'

The Professor of European History reeled.

'Stone me!' he cried. 'What kind of a question is that? We are looking at thirty-one little corpses!'

The Warden smiled, as only Wardens can.

'Call me an old academic quibbler if you will, Professor,' he murmured, 'but only *you* are looking at thirty-one little corpses.' He sighed a thoughtful sigh, and twitched his gown. '*I* am looking at thirty-one little vacancies.'

Shome Talk of Alexander

Alexander the Great was a great drunkard, according to a New York historian. Dr John O'Brien says that the talented Macedonian king exhibited the classic symp-'toms of acute alcoholism during his short life, and that drink caused his death at the age of 32.

Macedonians were noted for their liquor consump-tion, Dr O'Brien reports. Alexander's father, Philip, was a famous tippler, and his mother, Olympias, daughter of Neoptolemus of Epirus, was an enthusiastic disciple of Dionysus, god of wine. – The Times

Alexander III, called THE GREAT, king of Macedonia, was born in 356 BC, at Pella in Macedonia, two facts which escaped him for most of his short life. Drunk, he had great difficulty in working out how old he was, since (given that by the time he was twelve it was 344 BC) he seemed to be growing younger every year; nor could he clearly remember whether he had been born at Massa in Pelladonia or Poland in Alexandria. Asked for his name at parties, he frequently informed his hostess that he was Milton from Greater Pasadena. He would then fall down.

His father was Philip II, about which he was fairly clear, even if he didn't always get the number right; but as his mother was Olympias, daughter of Neoptolemus of Epirus, he never managed to refer to her as anything but Mrs II, unless it had been a really rough night, in which case she could be any number from Mrs I to XXXVI. However, as she was a heavy drinker herself, she never came when called, since this involved finding her other shoe.

Despite this, she was not as big a lush as her husband Philip, who wept most of the time, partly out of remorse, and partly because nobody would play *Melancholy Baby*; and it was because of this guilt-bred grief that Philip, deeply distressed by his son's inability to think straight, enunciate clearly, or, indeed, cross the room without knocking over the furniture, persuaded Aristotle, in 343 BC, to take Alexander on as a pupil.

It did not work out well: Pella was two hundred miles from Athens, and to get to Aristotle's place you had to change horses five times, plus make tight connections at Thebes-on-the-Hill and Sparta's End, where the buffet sold an unpretentious little retsina used mainly to despatch horses which had broken a leg en route. Because of this, young Alexander frequently ended up in Thrace, plastered, and shrieking at unimpressed citizens that he was the daughter of Mrs Aristotle IV and could lick anybody in the place.

Fortunately, the result of this early experience was that he became an expert swordsman, fearlessly prepared to take on six adversaries at a time. That everyone else saw only two adversaries does not, of course, diminish Alexander's heroism; in fact, the contrary. Indeed, such was his prowess that when Philip left with his army in 340 BC to attack Byzantium, he was confident to leave Alexander in charge of Macedonia; more confident, at least, than to take Alexander with him, since Alexander could not only not remember whether you turned left or right at the roundabout for Byzantium, he was unable to stay on his horse after a heavy breakfast.

While Philip was away, Alexander defeated the Maedi, a Thracian people; it was not a difficult victory, since the Maedi had been unaware that they were at war and were taken by surprise, but Philip was pleased with it, because any victory was a good excuse for a thrash. Three years later, however, the two fell out; when Philip divorced Olympias (the row is said to have begun over who had the corkscrew), Alexander fled with his mother to Epirus, since her father Neoptolemus lived in a forest, and 337 was a good year for wood alcohol.

But in 336, when Philip was assassinated (the reason is unclear, but the crime may not have been political, since Philip is known to have amassed a personal fortune of eighteen thousand empties which has never been found), Alexander succeeded him. He then marched south, in the hope of capturing the heavy aquavit plant in Norway, and found himself in Corinth, where he was appointed commander-in-chief of the Greek League, who took his halting Norse for colloquial Barbarian and elected him out of terror. Reeling into Thrace in the spring of 335, he found the bars shut and, in an invincible fury, crushed the bewildered Triballi before turning to cross the Danube, where he dispersed the Getae (for being out of stuffed olives). Meanwhile, a rumour of his death (he had been lying under a table for six days) had precipitated a revolt of Theban democrats. Waking, Alexander marched 240 miles in fourteen days, to Thebes. He still had the hangover, so Thebes was burned to the ground.

The Persian Expedition

From his accession, Alexander had set his mind on invading Persia, where, it was said, King Darius had discovered a method of distilling gin from dates which retailed at less than 3p a pint. At the River Granicus, Alexander stopped; the Persian plan was to tempt Alexander across (by telling him the first two drinks were on the house) and kill him in the melee, but the scheme misfired badly. Alexander, slumped between two satraps, had great difficulty in focusing on the heliograph, and interpreted the Persian invitation as a request to drink up and get out because it was closing time. Enraged, he hurled his forces across the river; the Persian line broke, exposing Asia Minor to the Macedonians. Most of the major cities opened their gates to Alexander, many of them throwing in a free ploughman's lunch, with the single exception of Miletus, which took courage from the fact that the Persian fleet lay close at hand. It was a mistake: Alexander did not attack the Persian fleet, as anticipated, since the movement of the ground beneath his feet led him to believe that he was *already afloat*; he thus attacked the coastal towns, under the impression they were large brick ships, and, stunned by this utterly unprecedented stratagem, they instantly surrendered. To his dying day, Alexander never understood why Miletus did not simply up anchor and sail away.

In the spring of 333 BC, Alexander subdued most of Asia Minor, and arrived in Gordium in Phrygia. It was here that he was presented with the Gordian knot, which according to legend could be loosed only by the man destined to rule Asia. Naturally unable to untie it (most days he could not even pick up his shoes, let alone find the laces), Alexander, in a fit of rage, cut through it with his sword. He also cut through his hat, his horse, his maps, and four bystanders, but it did not matter: all Persia lay at his feet, as, indeed, Alexander himself had so often done.

Conquest of Egypt

Wheeling south after the defeat of Darius, Alexander then marched west, though occasionally north, and once or twice in a circle, until, having subjugated Byblos and Sidon, he reached Tyre and put it under siege. The siege lasted seven months, and some historians maintain that it was the Tyrians who successfully resisted, when in fact it was rather that Alexander was forced to give up, because the tonic had run out. He took his army into Egypt, and founded Alexandria, erecting the huge Pharos lighthouse, one of the seven wonders of the world, so that he could find his way home at night.

History has it that it was in Alexandria that he began to think of himself as the son of Zeus. This is true, but it is also true that it was part of a painful delusory process brought on, ironically, by a tragic accident.

Alexander had lived all his short life in terror of delirium tremens, having seen what it could do to both his father and mother, who spent long periods of his childhood swatting one another under the mutual impression that the other was a giant spider. When he arrived in Egypt, the first thing he saw was a camel. He fainted. When he recovered, it was gone. Tentatively, he asked his aide-de-camp, Callisthenes, whether he had also seen 'that horse with the big knockers'. Callisthenes, not comprehending, suggested that Alexander switch brands; the general changed to Bloody Marys, but that night, staring at the Nile aimlessly, he saw his first alligator. He rushed, screaming, to his tent, where he told the distraught Callisthenes that he was being pursued by four-legged handbags.

Alexander subsequently refused, when it had dawned on everyone else, to believe the truth; those who claimed that they, too, had seen what he had seen were dismissed as flatterers, insulting him by humouring him. After he had killed twelve of these with a broken bottle, the rest stopped insisting that they were telling the truth; which finally satisfied their leader, while doing nothing to relieve his wretchedness.

He left Egypt, conquered Babylon in a somewhat depressed stupor, and pushed on towards India.

India and the Final Years

It was there that he saw his first elephant.

Next afternoon, in 328 BC, on the plains of Sogdiana, he met and immediately married a local girl, Roxana, daughter of King Oxyartes, because he didn't want to be alone at night when he woke up and saw the giant with the arm on its head walking around on four wastebins.

Unhappily, Roxana arrived for their wedding night riding on an elephant; forever thereafter, Alexander assumed that she, too, was a figment of his sodden imagination, and it came as no surprise to anyone when, four years later, he also married, at Susa, the daughter of his old adversary Darius. Inevitably, the two women fought over the dress allowance; Darius's daughter kept complaining to Alexander about his wife, from which Alexander inferred that his second wife was also either a drunk or a liar attempting to humour him, while Roxana kept complaining about his second wife, upon which Alexander would knock her about on the grounds that no figment of his imagination was going to tell him how to run his marriage.

There could be only one outcome of all this. Alexander took to drinking even more heavily, and, inevitably, early in 323, he failed, one morning to rise from his bed. Friends continued to throw water over him for eight days, but it did no good, any more.

Slim Chance

Twenty years at the Olivetti, five million words, many of them different, and I never wrote about smoking or diet.

What is this sentence?

A testimonial to be handed in at the Pearly Gates, while I hop from one foot to the other and wait with a chewed lip (if they have feet and lips There) for the committee to decide between harps and tridents?

An attempt to wheedle the Sun Alliance quack into turning a kindly ophthalmoscope upon my mortgage extension request? ('The applicant is a humorist who has never written about smoking or diet, ergo he neither smokes nor eats, throw the bugger another fiver.')

An oleaginous bid to charm Olivetti into kicking in with a replacement, given that after five million words the platen is as graven as a Mosaic tablet and the £ flies across the room when struck in anger ('SIR, THIS RIDICULOUS GAS BILL FOR *PING!* . . .)?

No.

This sentence (i.e. *that* sentence, a foot or so of words having now elapsed) is the first sentence of an article about diet. The other sentences (i.e. between *that* and *this*) are to cover the embarrassment of writing it.

I do so only as a public service. You will have seen, of course, that every other major newspaper and magazine (with, as I recall, the exception of *The Embalmer*) has in recent weeks given over much of its columnage to diet advice. There are two main reasons for this: it is summer, when people wish to look their best in raincoats and balaclavas; and second, it is not possible for anyone to do anything about anything any more, viz. remove the Russians from Afghanistan, remove the hostages from

Iran, remove the Government to somewhere with rubber walls, and so on. Faced with a world which has rendered us impotent – we cannot even stop Graham Gooch flashing at rising balls outside the off stump – man has increasingly turned to those areas over which he does retain control, i.e. cutting down to five a day and losing half a stone. Several have bought cycling machines.

When the Russians take out Molesworth, we shall simply turn our faces from the flash and, lung-clean and skinny, pedal motionlessly away.

Leading the file of jogging lard as it gasps up Fleet Street is *The Sunday Times*: not only have they come up with their own diet sheets, not only have they thereto appended recipes and other kitchenhold hints, not only have they coerced four eminent fatties, including the world's largest peer, into volunteering as guinea pigs, they have also leaned on a number of restaurants to join a mutual promotion stunt wherein the restaurateurs now offer a Sunday Times Menu, although this may be nothing more than a timely sop to the NGA, since a glance at the restaurants mentioned suggests that only compositors could afford to eat there.

Clearly, *Punch*, ever in the vogue vanguard, could not be caught with its trousers down; or, rather, with its trousers swelling at the seams. And since I myself have, in the past four weeks, slimmed astonishingly down from an unhealthy thirteen stone three to a totally debilitated twelve stones, I felt it my duty to pass on the fruits, unsweetened, of this wonderful experience. There will also be diet sheets, kitchen hints, advice on exercise, and a free extra bonus on cigarette-reduction. There will, however, be no list of Punch-linked restaurants, but anyone writing to this office and including a stamped addressed envelope will receive a list of cheap stone-masons.

THE PUNCH DIET: SOME PRELIMINARY NOTES
I have been on a low-carbohydrate, low-cholesterol,

low-protein, low-liquid diet; since nutritional experts appear to disagree on everything, it seemed best to cut out food. I have designated it the low-spirit diet, or, because it is slimmer, LSD. As it is also unnervingly expensive, we have a happy coincidence there. It is the only happy thing we have. I get no butter, eggs, milk, sugar, fried items, cheese, bread, potatoes... I am starting from the wrong end. The senescent Olivetti will not cope with the list of what I don't get. What I get is Swedish ceiling-board, a little sunflower oil, and water. Sometimes there are tiny fragments of fish in the water. Birthdays, I get a slice of lemon in it. Every Coronation Day, I am allowed a stick of celery.

The fact that I have lost seventeen pounds in four weeks, though, is not, I am certain, entirely attributable to this appalling regimen; mainly, it is to do with converting the fat I already had into energy, and this cranking up of the metabolic engineering was achieved, and I stress this urgently, as a direct result of *attempting* to diet.

PRE-BREAKFAST

Most diet sheets start with breakfast. That is their error. Slimming begins the moment you wake. Pre-breakfast, on the *Punch* diet, you weigh yourself. This involves, since the bedroom carpet is an unreliable base, standing the weighing-machine on the (closed) lavatory, and climbing on it, using a deep breath, a small heave, and the handle of the cistern. As you grow slimmer, you may be able to dispense with the handle. Simply dragging your adipose ruins aboard the scales, do you see, has already expended invaluable milligrams; early on in your diet, you will find that the scales frequently slide off the lid while you are dragging yourself onto it, thereby forcing you to repeat the exercise, often losing many more grams in sponging forehead blood off the bidet, etc. Once on the scales, remove heavy items like wedding rings, yesterday's forehead Elastoplast, navel-lint, and so forth: individually, they may look little, but collectively could add up to several more grams, especially if your wedding-ring, as you fall from the slid scales, rolls under the bath. Crawling after it on nothing more than yesterday's Ryvita could expend anything up to an ounce.

This I usually follow with a little screaming. Feel the heart race! Pump, pump, pump goes the little fellow as you get those nasty waste thoughts out of your system, burning fat as you go.

Clean the teeth vigorously. The weight of plaque is often under-estimated. Shave close. Doesn't that pile of heavy bristles in the basin look *good*?

BREAKFAST
Half a cup of black coffee, no sugar
Watch the children eat four rashers, two eggs, porridge, and six slices of toast. Look at their happy, full faces! Don't you want to reach out and clout them? Well, that's a *good* feeling, on the *Punch* diet: rage is even better than screaming for metabolizing fat.

Don't forget skimmed fat-free milk. The milkman always does. Running after his dwindling float and shouting 'What about my bloody skimmed milk?' is a wonderful way to slimness and health.

ELEVENSES
What! I hear you cry. *Elevenses*? Well, not as fatties know them. At eleven o'clock, talk to the people in your office, school, chambers, hospital, pit-face, or wherever, about your diet. Tell them how many milligrams you lost last night, tell them how many stairs you can run up now without gasping, tell them how many old suits now fit you again. They will run away from you. Run after them, shouting as you run. Shout about Perrier water or

Flora. It is marvellous exercise, toning up calves, thighs, and jaws.

Half a cup of black coffee, no sugar
Slice of crispbread
Radish

Drink the black coffee. Eat the crispbread. Sticks in the throat, doesn't it? Don't you wish you'd saved some of the coffee, now? Throw the radish.

After lunch, it is time for your first cigarette of the day. Take it out of the packet. Stare at it. Put it back in the packet. If you have been on thirty a day heretofore, you will find yourself biting your knuckles, a wonderful toner-up of flabby chins and neglected forearms. The rest of your lunch hour could profitably be spent in running after all the colleagues you didn't see at eleven o'clock and trying to tell them about giving up cigarettes.

Alternatively, why not visit a health food shop? Do not buy anything; just because it is full of nourishing mouse-droppings and organic bacteria does not make the stuff slimming. But get into an argument with an assistant. You will find that the skinny young swine is all too happy to explain to you about the presence of the godhead in yak yogurt, and may pursue you for miles, ringing his little bell. This is called Reverse Elevenses.

TEA TIME

Yes, it's true. Around four o'clock, you will almost certainly, if the *Punch* diet has been assiduously followed, feel as though a man has come to dismantle your head with a coke-hammer. Now is the time to take a high tea of four aspirin in a bouillon of lightly poured water. Aspirin contains no calories, and, taken regularly on an empty stomach, will rot holes in your alimentary canal, allowing any food inadvertently taken to fall through. You might also be fortunate enough to end up on a surgical ward, where the food is utterly inedible.

DINNER
Shredded white cabbage
Two slices crispbread
Large tumbler neat water
Sultana (or raisin)
Half a cup of black coffee, no sugar

In the *Punch* diet, an electric vegetable shredder is invaluable. Try to find one where the nut securing the drive shaft falls out. Then walk or run to the nearest stockist. In my own case, this was Stuttgart, so I had to compromise by running to a place that *looked* as though it might stock it, since it stocked every other bloody piece of electric rubbish. Then bang on the door. Then look at your watch. Then run home again. A wonderful exercise for legs and fatty fists and lungs. As soon as your fists are less fatty, you can begin, on your way home, punching fools daring to stare at you for talking to yourself.

Shredding the cabbage by hand, it is simplicity itself to lose a thumb weighing anything up to four ounces. Remember, for your health's sake, to use fresh coffee, ground at home. A tin of Blue Mountain, slipping from your cabbage-slimy and enfeebled fingers, will bring hundreds of little beans bouncing all over the kitchen floor, a wonderful exercise for flattening those podgy knees!

SLEEP

Needless to say, it is very important to get as little sleep as possible. Asleep, our metabolic rate goes down, there is nobody to shriek at, no way of burning nervous energy, and no means of crossing half bloody London trying to buy a cycling machine only to find they have just sold the one you reserved over the phone.

On the *Punch* diet, you lie awake wondering whether you're going crazy. Sometimes you worry whether a burglar has just torn through a partition wall or whether it was only your stomach grinding in its endless poignant hunt for an errant crumb. Sometimes you see fat lamb chops walking across the ceiling explaining to jacket potatoes that they now smoke forty a day.

The only cure for this is to get up and weigh yourself. Trying to find a wedding-ring under the bath in the dark, you could be well on the way to living forever.

Not a Lot of it About

Free sex will soon be available on the National Health Service, it was claimed yesterday. Dr Martin Cole predicted that substitute lovers will be prescribed for patients with bedroom hang-ups. He believes that other doctors are now coming round to the view that making love with a stand-in husband or wife does help cure problems. – The Sun

Mr Kevin Dunmoe limped heavily into the waiting-room, eased himself onto one of the wormy bentwood chairs with a heroically muted groan, stretched his right leg out in front of him with both hands, and smiled the smile of the damaged brave.

There was, of course, nothing wrong with his leg. But, in his frequent visits to his GP down the long arches of the years with his myriad minor malfunctions, the head colds, the whitlows, the aches, the corns, the alopecia, the passing quirks of ear and sphincter, Mr Dunmoe had invariably chosen a waiting-room persona which suggested that his right leg had come off at the hip, but that his upper lip was taking this in its stride. Once, when a small boil beneath his left arm had refused to come to a head, he had turned up in crutches and a rudimentary neckbrace fashioned from a raspberry cloche.

Today, in particular, his ailment required subterfuge of a high order. The leg would ward off risky solicitude. Even so, a pre-emptive strike might be wise. He turned, wincing, to the large middle-aged woman beside him.

'I see,' he said, 'that your little boy has got his head stuck in a saucepan.' He tapped the utensil with his knuckle. 'Who's been a silly little fellow, then?'

'NYONG!' cried the saucepan. 'BOYNG!'

'What did the little lad say?' enquired Dunmoe.

'He said *Sod off,*' replied the woman.

'Dear, dear!' said Dunmoe. 'How old is he?'

'Forty-three,' said the woman.

Dunmoe stared at her.

'But he's got shorts on!' he exlaimed. 'He has got two badges for woodcraft. He has got a jack-knife and a woggle.'

'That,' said the woman, 'is part of his treatment. You nosey bastard,' she added.

'Are you his mum?'

'I am his wife. As you're here, would you like your other leg broken?'

The waiting-room door opened.

'Mr Dunmoe?' enquired the receptionist.

Dunmoe got up, with dramatic difficulty, and followed her into the dark green corridor. She stared at his stiff leg.

'Bit of cramp,' said Dunmoe, straightening up.

She led him into the doctor's surgery. The doctor glanced up from baggy eyes, and down again.

'Mr Dunmoe,' he said.

'There's a bloke out there with his head in a saucepan,' said Dunmoe. 'Also, he is a boy scout from the neck down.'

'I have a number of sexual cases, Mr Dunmoe,' murmured the doctor, 'now, if you'll just go behind...'

'Oh,' said Dunmoe. 'Ah. Got you. He, er, he likes something a...'

'I do not discuss my patients,' said the doctor. He wound his propelling-pencil lead up, and then down again, slowly. 'What is this time, Mr Dunmoe? Colic? Chaps? A terminal blackhead?'

'As a matter of fact,' said the patient, drawing his chair an inch or two closer to the desk, 'it is the other. Not, I hasten to add, anything involving saucepans, nothing of that order, it is a fairly straightforward case of, er, thing.'

'Thing?'

'Basically, what I am suffering from might be described as not enough.'

'I see.'

'It is now May, practically June, and if I tell you Boxing Day, and a possible near miss on February 11, if my memory serves me right, I assume I do not have to draw pictures? Also, Boxing Day she was knitting throughout.'

'Knitting?'

'A bed jacket for the cat. You see where the priorities lie, I take it?'

'What do you expect me to do, Mr Dunmoe?'

Dunmoe cleared his throat.

'I pay my stamp regular,' he said. 'I expect to get a prescription. Also a certificate for off work, due to where I shall need to be in bed, I assume, unless it is a matter of doing it on the premises at Boot's, which I should definitely not prefer, what with people coming in for Gee's linctus etcetera all the time, also staring at you from the weighing machine.'

The doctor sighed, and pushed his prescription pad around his desk.

'I take it you have discussed this with Mrs Dunmoe?'

'I hardly see her. She is up cat obedience classes all day. The bugger will not get into his bed jacket. That is possibly what is giving her all these nocturnal migraines, wouldn't you say?'

'I really have no idea.'

Dunmoe sniffed.

'Makes no odds, anyway. I have definitely gone off her. It really come home to me when I got a lift up here on his truck from my mate Brian and I realized how unattractive my old woman was by comparison.'

The doctor glanced up, a small gleam of professional interest lighting his eye for the first time.

'You mean,' he said, 'that you find Mrs Dunmoe less attractive than your friend Brian?'

'No,' said Dunmoe, 'I find her less attractive than his truck.'

The doctor stared at Dunmoe for a while, chewing his lip. It had been a long day, and it wasn't over yet. There was old Mrs Rapaport and her insatiable need for lollipop men to sort out, there was the not inconsiderable diagnostic hurdle of Detective Inspector Wimbley and his parrot Russell, there was the postmistress whose husband had taken to hanging upside down from the shower-rail and who was now insisting on her right to a free NHS wooden stake and mallet, to say nothing of the man in the saucepan. So he sighed, and he scribbled on his pad, and he ripped the prescription off, and he handed it to Dunmoe, who took it and ran, in his haste almost knocking over the incoming patient; who appeared, to his fleeting eye, to be a Merino sheep in a gymslip and pith helmet.

'Yes?' enquired the pebble-eyed girl at the chemist's prescription counter.

Dunmoe pushed his crumpled paper across, awkwardly.

'I was, er, I was rather hoping for a man,' he muttered.

'That's not what it says here,' said the girl, scrutinising the scrawl. 'Your doctor is doubtless trying to wean you off 'em.'

'I didn't mean that,' whispered Dunmoe.

'It says here,' said the girl doggedly, 'small rat-head with – God almighty, some of them have appalling writing! What's that say?'

'I'm not sure, I –'

'Give us it!' cried a large woman beside Dunmoe, who was waiting to pay for an elastic stocking and a pelican bib. She put on her glasses. 'Small red-head, that is. Small red-head with lard bust.'

'Large bust,' hissed Dunmoe, gripping the counter. 'Large bust.'

The salesgirl turned, slid back a ribbed glass partition, and shouted:

'Mr Dennison, we got any of them big-busted little red-heads in stock?'

Most of the customers looked round. Dunmoe closed his eyes. When he opened them again, the pharmacist's head was poking through the hatch.

'No, Doreen,' he said. 'I'll have to get one made up.'

'You'll have to wait,' said Doreen to Dunmoe.

'I'll take anything!' cried Dunmoe, his neck reddening. 'Blonde, brunette, you name it. I do not wish to hang about all day, narmean?'

The pharmacist stared at him, and back at Doreen.

'Some people!' he cried. Several customers nodded. 'Take anything, he says! He does not appreciate that mine is a skilled profession, Doreen.'

'Could kill him, a blonde,' said Doreen. 'Some people!'

'Took me three bloody years to qualify!' shouted the pharmacist at Dunmoe. He hurled the partition shut. The ribbed glass cracked.

Dunmoe, hotfaced, walked away, accentuating his limp, feigning interest in a display of trusses. Customers whispered. After some fifteen minutes, his name was called, very loudly, and he looked up.

The pharmacist was approaching with a short dumpy woman in a bright red wig and an asymmetrical bosom.

'Bloody hell!' cried Dunmoe. 'Can I have it in a bag?'

'You shut your face!' shrieked the prescription. 'You are bloody lucky to get me.'

'She can go like a bomb, under the right conditions,' said the pharmacist.

The prescription stared at Kevin Dunmoe.

'Fat chance,' she said.

'Once a night,' said the pharmacist, 'with a glass of water. It is dangerous to exceed the stated dose.'

'Dangerous?' cried Dunmoe. 'It is bloody impossible!'

'Come on,' said the prescription, 'you got to get my dinner ready.'

'What?'

The prescription passed Dunmoe a green voucher.

'That,' she said, 'is a DHSS chitty entitling me to a hot

dinner, to include soup and a choice of pudding. You tear off your half and claim it back via Swansea. I do not eat pork, by the way, it gives me wind.'

Dunmoe thrust his way through the chemist's, limping appallingly, biting his lip, the prescription clacketing after him on her broken heels, and pushed out into the street.

At the bus stop, an idea suddenly occurred to him.

'Here,' he said, 'funny thing, I suddenly feel a lot better! I could very well have undergone a miraculous cure. Well, well! My, my! I'll be saying goodbye, then.'

'I should cocoa,' said the prescription. 'I do not get mucked about, sunshine. There's laws. You could get done for malingering, false declaration, wasting public time and money, all that. You could also get a kick in the slats. You do not slide out of your hot dinner commitments that easy, son, also roof over my head for seven nights, catch my drift?'

Bitterly, Dunmoe limped aboard the bus. The prescription followed him upstairs. They sat down together, behind another couple. Dunmoe gasped.

It was the man with the saucepan over his head. Beside him sat a tall, lissome, Chanel-wafting natural blonde, clinging to the patient's arm. Dunmoe leaned forward, and peered. She had the best legs he had ever seen in his life, the dimpled knees just visible beyond the gleamingly cream *balcon* of her decolletage.

Dunmoe banged on the saucepan.

'How?' he cried. 'How?'

'UNGYUNG!' replied the saucepan. 'MYOING! CLANG!'

'What did he say?' shrieked Dunmoe.

'He said,' murmured the blonde, her voice like molten gold, 'that he decided to go privately.'

The Young Man and the Sea

A tall story about a record-breaking stuffed tarpon failed to impress at Sotheby's yesterday, where it sold for £190. The golden-coloured fish, mounted on a board and estimated at £500, was among the highlights of a sporting sale, and was indisputably six feet eight-and-a-half inches long.

But whether it was caught, as inscribed, by Ernest Hemingway in 1902 was in some doubt, as the writer was only four years old at the time. – Daily Telegraph

In the spring, the potty was still there, but I did not go to it any more. It had been one of the good potties, but the thing with the potties was over, now.

Now I went to the big one with the lid. You lifted the lid, and then you lifted the round one with the hole in it that was under the lid, and then you took aim, and when the aim was good you did not have the bad thing with the shoe. Some of the time you would worry about what might happen if the lid fell and you got a wound in that place where it was very bad to have a wound, but you did not worry about that all of the time, because if you worried about that all of the time you would have to keep looking at the lid, and then you would have the bad thing with the shoe.

I came down the stairs, and I went into the room where the man and the woman were having breakfast. There was a smell of coffee in the room. When the coffee pot stood on the stove, it got hot, and a smell of coffee came out of it. That is the way it is with coffee. The man did not look up from his newspaper. Only the woman looked at me.

142

'What have you got in your mouth?' she said.

'I hag nog gog anyging ing my moug,' I said.

The woman held out her hand.

'Give me the thing from your mouth,' she said.

I took the thing from my mouth and I put it in her hand.

'What is the thing from his mouth?' said the man.

'It is a glass eye,' said the woman.

'Why does he have a glass eye in his mouth?' said the man.

The woman looked at me again.

'Why do you have a glass eye in your mouth?' she said.

'It is the eye of my bear,' I said. 'The bear was on my bed this morning. It was downwind of me. I hit the bear with a left, but when it did not go down, I knew I was in for a fight. I hit it with two more left jabs, but it was not until I hit it with my right cross that its eye fell out.'

The man put down his paper.

'It was a bear of much *cojones*,' he said.

'It was a bear of very little brain,' said the woman. 'If someone throws you two left jabs, you can be sure that what is coming next is the right cross. Ask your father about the night of the Macombers' cocktail party.'

The man looked out of the window.

'It was not your right cross that got me,' he said. 'I blocked your right cross. I am always ready for your right cross. What got me on the night of the Macombers' cocktail party was your left hook.'

The man stood up, and went out.

'Was that the way it was?' I said.

'No,' said the woman. 'The right cross was the way it was. That is why he cannot remember any more. It was a good right cross. The earth moved for him.'

'Can you fix a bear?' I said.

The woman shook her head.

'You cannot fix a bear after it has a bad wound,' she said. 'It would always have a squint. It is not easy, the thing with the needle and the thread. Especially when you have the thing with the bottle. It was a brave bear, and it would not be fair on it. I shall throw it in the trash.'

143

'Can I have a dog instead?' I said.

'No,' she said. 'You are not ready to fight a dog yet. A dog would fight back. You could get a wound, down there.'

'If you got me a gun as well,' I said, 'that would even things up. I could shoot the dog.'

The woman thought about this for a while.

'I will think about this for a while,' she said. She looked at me. 'Do not put egg in your ear.'

She moistened a handkerchief, and she cleaned out my ear. I went on to the back porch. It was one of those sharp spring mornings you only get in Oak Park, Illinois, with a clean crisp smell coming off the Des Plaines River and blending with the faint odour of gin from your ear. A lark sang, rising, and I looked around quickly, but I could not find the right kind of stone, so I walked out of the yard, and down to the corner of the street, where the old one sat, blinking at the sunlight, the way he always did.

'Hallo, old one,' I said.

The old one looked up at me, and smiled. He had no teeth. The day before he had had one tooth, but even that was gone, now.

'I am sorry about the tooth, old one,' I said.

He shrugged.

'That is the way it is when you are seven,' he said. 'You will find it out for yourself soon enough, young one. But it is not so bad. The fairy came and gave me a dime for it.'

'I hope the fairy will look after me when my time comes, old one,' I said.

'The thing is to be a good one while you are a young one,' said the old one. 'That way she will come when you are an old one.'

I looked at the ground. There was an ant, doing what ants do. I wanted to step on the ant very much, but I was afraid the fairy would see, so instead I said:

'Do you want to play, old one?'

He smiled that same black and empty smile.

'It is not for the old ones to play with the young ones,' he said.

'I thought we would do the thing with the doorbells,' I said. 'I thought we would do the thing where we ring the doorbells and we run away. You used to be the very best there was at the thing with the doorbells, old one.'

The old one traced a pattern in the dirt with his finger.

'That was a long time ago, young one,' he said.

He did not say any more after that, because a girl came by, and these were not things discussed in front of those who are not like men and who are not troubled with the danger of the lid.

'What are you doing?' she said.

'*Nada*,' said the old one. '*Nada y nada y nada.*'

'What does that mean?' said the girl.

'I do not know,' said the old one. 'There is this book I saw at school. It is called *¡Hola, Pepe!* All the punctuation is upside down. These words were in it.'

'Perhaps they mean '*the punctuation is upside down*', old one?' I said.

The old one shrugged again.

'Who can say?' he said. 'Soon they will teach me, and I will pass it on to you, young one, and then you will know. It is my duty.'

'He is truly a great one,' said the girl. 'No wonder he gets such a good price for his teeth.'

I nodded.

'Would you like to play doctors and nurses?' I said.

She shook her head.

'Why do you not wish to play doctors and nurses with the young one?' enquired the old one.

'I do not like the way he plays it,' said the girl. 'It is a bad way.'

The old one looked at me, and back to the girl.

'Why bad?'

'He makes me bandage him from head to foot,' said the girl, 'and I have to feed him through a little tube where his mouth is, and then he asks me over and over again

145

when he will be well enough to go back to the front. It can take hours.'

She went off, skipping.

'I obscenity in the obscenity of her obscenity, and no returns,' I said.

The old one sighed.

'Leave me now, young one,' he said, 'I wish to be alone with my thoughts. Tomorrow, we have the thing with the tens and the units.'

'I understand, old one,' I said. 'I, too, have to be on my way. I am seeking an animal to replace my bear. They say I am too young for a dog, and I know I am too old, now, for a toy. It will not be easy.'

'*Hola Pepe y Hola Pepe y Hola Pepe,*' murmured the old one. 'Nothing is easy. But perhaps I have a solution, young one. I know where there is a giant fish, bigger than a man, which is not a toy but neither is it alive. In its day, it was a very brave one, young one. I think it would be right for you. But it is much money.'

I felt my blood turn, with that mixture of fear and elation that you have when you pick up a telephone and dial a number and when the person answers you make a noise like the wind breaking and ring off again.

'Where is this great fish?' I said.

'It is in the window of the place that is called Sam's Loan and Pawn,' said the old one. 'Go with God.'

I ran all the way, with my heart beating in my throat, and I fell into the shop, and I saw the giant fish which was indeed bigger than a man, hanging above the counter, and I pointed to it, breathless, unable to speak.

'I am afraid,' said Sam, 'that the tarpon is fifty bucks, small one.'

I dug into my pocket, and I pulled out a dead frog, and half a Hershey bar, and an old cartridge case, and a mouse-trap, and a broken knife, and six marbles, and a hundred-dollar bill.

Sam took the bill, and held it up to the light, and looked at me.

'Where did you get this?' he said.

146

'From the *Saturday Evening Post*,' I said. 'I write stories.'

'I do not understand, small one,' said Sam, but he put the money in the till and he gave me five tens change, 'I do not understand how a four-year-old one sells stories to the *Post*. Forgive me, but you have only very simple thoughts, and you know only very short words.'

I took the fish down, and I put it on my shoulder.

'That is where the money is,' I said.

Box Pop

'Baird then set up in business, marketing successively a patent sock, jam, honey, and soap... following a complete nervous breakdown, he retired to Hastings in 1922 and decided to concentrate upon television, which had been the dream of scientists for fifty years. Baird occupied an attic at 8 Queen's Arcade and, having very little capital, assembled his crude makeshift apparatus on a washstand. The base of his motor was a tea-chest, a biscuit tin housed the projection lamp, scanning discs were cut from cardboard, and fourpenny cycle lenses were utilized. Scrap-wood, darning needles, string, and sealing-wax held the apparatus together.' – Dictionary of National Biography

The Patents Officer peered through the brass spy-hole, into the waiting-room.

'Stone me!' he muttered. 'It's only bloody him again!'

He slid the spy-hole cover shut; and patted it. It was a nice little number, that. The nice little number, in fact, was Pat. No. 9078649, and it was down to him, the spy-hole's inventor having, by great good fortune, slipped on the office staircase and broken his neck. Life was a matter of snapping up opportunities, in the Patents Officer's considered view. Year or two, he'd be able to open a boarding-house on the royalties; Bexhill, Frinton, somewhere like that, put his feet up.

'Only bloody who?' enquired the Assistant Patents Officer, throwing a coke-fired family nose-wiper into the waste-bin and addressing his screwdriver to a luminous hat.

148

'Logie's Electric Socks,' said the PO.

'God Almighty!' cried his assistant. 'I remember testing them, they was supposed to keep your feet snug in all weathers. I was crossing Waterloo Bridge when it come on to rain, they short-circuited and blew me brown brogues into the bloody river.' He dismembered a clockwork denture, savagely. 'Beats me why you give him a patent on them buggers.'

The PO sniffed.

'I reckoned if he killed enough people, they'd lock him up. Get him out of our hair. Remember that cock-up over his jam and soap?'

'Need you ask!' said the APO, holding a mouse-strangler up to the light and squinting at it. 'It wasn't until I'd granted the patent that I twigged about which one I was supposed to have tested and which one I was supposed to have washed with.'

'Hardly your fault, Stanley,' said his senior. 'You don't often come across carbolic jam.'

'Or raspberry soap,' said Stanley. He jabbed his bradawl into an inflatable cardigan, and the windows rattled. 'What's he brought this time?'

The Patents Officer sneaked a second squint through his pension.

'Tea-chest with a biscuit tin on it,' he said. 'Seems to be held together by sealing-wax. Got lamps, mind.'

'Could be anything,' said Stanley. He lashed out expertly with his mallet, and a glass briefcase flew into disappointing fragments. 'Travelling Turkish bath, pet incinerator, personalized gun emplacement. You know him. Has he done a death-ray yet?'

'Not to my knowledge,' replied the PO.

'That'll be it, then,' said Stanley. 'Last ten tea-chests with biscuit tins on have been death-rays. Shall we let him in, get it over with?'

'Might as well,' said the Patents Officer. 'It's either that or him having another nervous breakdown in the waiting-room. Can't risk that, with half a dozen bloody robots sitting out there just asking to be set off by a sudden noise. Last thing you want of a Tuesday morning is a load of robots suddenly jumping about, springs everywhere, cogs getting in the Hoover.'

Stanley opened the door.

'Next!'

John Logie Baird lurched into the room, dragging his invention behind him. His eyes were wild, his hair was straggled, his tie was under his ear.

'Right, Mr Baird,' said the Patents Officer, licking his pencil, 'what is it this time? Raspberry death-ray? Thing for turning socks into honey?'

'It's a televisor,' said Baird hoarsely. 'It sends pictures by radio.'

'Get your hammer, Stanley,' said the Patents Officer.

Baird shrieked weakly, and threw his frail arms around the tea-chest. The Patents Officer's hand stayed his assistant in mid-swing; the risk of a nervous collapse was too great, there would be questions, forms to fill out, disruption. They might be forced to redecorate. He sighed.

'Perhaps, Mr Baird,' he said, 'you would be kind enough to demonstrate?'

Baird began to separate the giant contraption into two different elements; he plugged the tea-chest into a wall-socket. It started to hum, and to chatter, and to glow; a smell not unlike roast goose slowly filled the office.

'This is the receiver,' he explained, tapping it. It wobbled, coughed. 'The other is the transmitter, which I shall take into the next room.'

'Hang on,' said Stanley, 'we've got our sandwiches in there.'

'It's perfectly safe,' said Baird, lugging it after him through the door. A sprocket-wheel followed him for a yard or so, then rolled under a filing cabinet.

'Watch the screen!' called Baird.

The two officials stared at the tiny flickering window in the tea-chest. After a moment or two, Baird's thin face, somewhat distorted, grew dimly visible on it. The mouth moved, and the converted foghorn nailed to the lid began to crackle.

'Four people fell off the roof this morning,' it said, through the static, 'and they're all dead. John Logie Baird, News at Ten, Lewisham High Street.'

The wobbling face disappeared, and Baird himself came back into the office.

'What was all that about?' enquired the Patents Officer.

'It was the news,' said Baird.

''Get off!' cried the Assistant Patents Officer. 'I come down Lewisham High Street this morning, there was nobody jumping off nothing.'

'It was just an example,' muttered Baird wretchedly, 'of what television can do.'

'Oh was it?' said the PO. 'Well, you get a bloody sight more in the *Daily Sketch*, mate. *And* it's only a ha'penny.'

The inventor glared at them for a while. Then he turned, and went back next door.

'WOULD ONE OF YOU COME IN HERE, PLEASE?' he shouted.

They looked at one another.

'Go on, Stanley,' said the Patents Officer.

'Sod off,' said his assistant.

The Patents Officer sucked his teeth.

'Do not force me to pull rank, son,' he said.

Stanley walked slowly to the door.

'If anything happens to this suit,' he said darkly, 'I am holding you personally responsible.'

Nothing happened for some time. The tea-chest began to throb ominously. The Patents Officer looked at his watch. Then, from next door, came his assistant's voice, uncharacteristically quavering.

'HE WANTS ME TO BE MARY PICKFORD!' called Stanley.

'I'll come in,' shouted the Patents Officer, leaping up.

'NO!' shrieked Baird. He slammed the door, and locked it.

'Oy!' cried the Patents Officer. 'I do not want nothing untoward going on in there. Is he dressed, Stanley? This is Government property.'

'WATCH THE SCREEN!' howled Baird through the wall.

The Patents Officer sat down again. There were two shadowy figures on the tea-chest window now, sitting down facing one another.

'Hello, good evening, and welcome,' said the foghorn. 'The first guest on my show tonight is that great star of the silver screen, Miss Mary Pickford! Mary, tell me, what is it *really* like, being married to Douglas Fairbanks?'

The tiny figure of Stanley got up.

'Shut your face,' said the foghorn.

The door was unlocked, and the two men came back into the office.

'Did I miss something?' said the Patents Officer.

'It was a chat show,' said Baird. 'Glamour, romance, wit. All that.'

'He's round the twist,' said the sweating Stanley. 'How could they tell when he was having a nervous breakdown, that's what I'd like to know.'

'If I want Mary Pickford,' said the Patents Officer to Baird, 'I go up the Blue Hall, Islington. Piano, packet of crisps, nice big women sitting on their own. You get the plot, mounties, usually a clever dog, people tied to railway lines. Something to get your teeth into. I don't want to see her one inch high on a bleeding tea-chest, telling me what she had for dinner. I don't call that entertainment.'

Baird clasped his forehead, reeling.

'But with my televisor,' he cried, 'you wouldn't *have* to go out! You could sit there with your wife, feet up on the –'

'Oh lovely!' said the Patents Officer. 'She takes her teeth out, evenings. Seven o'clock, I'm gone, son. Down the Rat & Cockle, nice pint of Bass in front of me, dartboard waiting, know what I mean?'

'Look!' shouted Baird desperately. 'Just give me one

more chance. I'll *prove* what a marvellous boon to mankind this is, just come next door with me, I'll –'

'Your turn,' said Stanley, smirking. 'Only fair.'

'Keep the door open,' said the Patents Officer.

'Watch the screen,' said Baird.

Stanley sat down at the tea-chest. After a moment or two, Baird and the PO materialized, thinly.

' . . . a Patents Officer from Hounslow. His special subject is the history of China. You have two minutes, starting from now. How tall is –'

There was a bang. Black smoke began to drift across the seated couple. 'I've started,' said Baird, 'so I'll finish. How tall is Sun Yat Sen?'

There was a second bang. The screen went blank.

Baird and the Patents Officer came back into the office. Their faces were black. Most of their hair had gone.

'We apologize for the break in transmission,' murmured Baird to Stanley, 'normal service will –'

'Get him out of here, Stanley,' muttered the Patents Officer.

'But you don't understand!' cried Baird, as he and the tea-chest were shoved rapidly through the door. 'Some day, millions of people –'

'Next!' called Stanley.

Drink to me Only

The Sun

WEDNESDAY, DECEMBER 24

Knock off twelve noon, i.e. eleven a.m. on account of agreed wash-up time, i.e. ten a.m. due to Lucky Draw procedures as laid down at branch level and duly ratified nem con, i.e. 9.30 a.m. owing to time allowed after frank and free negotiations with management for putting on cotton-wool beard and gum-boots, i.e. nine a.m. on account of agreed post-clocking-on wash-up time to remove dangerous muck getting on hands from time clock.

Draw Lucky Draw; win Lucky Draw as laid down in standing orders; £67.50, i.e. better than a poke in the eye with a sharp stick, repair to Rat & Cockle at 10.30 a.m. with Big Brian, Jeff, Little Brian, Eric, Kevin, Irish Brian, the Other Jeff and Brian. Drank Lucky Draw.

Come out three o'clock, fall over gravel bin, Big Brian sick on Little Brian, Jeff and the Other Jeff playing leapfrog up Pontefract Crescent, the Other Jeff only falls through Tesco's window. Seasonally reduced turkey giblets all over him. Kevin starts screaming on account of he interprets it as the Other Jeff's bowels have dropped out due to broken glass etcetera, police very sympathetic, bang Kevin's head on the Panda.

Crawl home 6 p.m., Sharon opens door in fetching Scotcade negligée and new blonde hairpiece, looks like escaped lion they only just got the net over in time. Sharon got hold of magnum of sparkling rosé plus peculiar look in eye, also that shiny stuff on lips, it looks like she's just finished eating a lard brick. Yours truly's reaction is oh bloody hell, there she goes up the stairs, there is no question but she is after a bit, can it be Christmas already? Coming, my darling, I call, walk into hatstand, fall down, start going up stairs.

Wake up on stairs. It is five a.m.

THURSDAY, DECEMBER 25

Wake up again, this time in bed, it is 9 a.m., feels like skull fractured in eighteen places. Happy Christmas beloved I forgive you murmurs Sharon, yours truly's reaction is oh bloody hell, there is no escape this time, but door bursts open.

It is Tracy (7) and Osvaldo Burt (6), our eldest. They are screaming and bashing one another with Eamonn Terry Melvyn (2), our youngest, due to where Tracy has stepped on Osvaldo Burt's new Space Invaders electronic game (£23.95, but not any more it bloody isn't), and Osvaldo Burt has jumped on Tracy's new Sindy Doll (£6.95, not including one eye popped out, leg torn off, and bum on backwards).

Sharon leaps out of bed shrieking and lashing out with gift-wrapped Bex-Bissell carpet shampooer (not particularly romantic, I never said it was, but it's better than treading on hamster droppings when you're walking about in bare feet looking for the Alka-Seltzer).

I seize the opportunity to get up sharpish and dress. My view is once I've got my trousers on and lathered my face, Sharon will come to her senses.

Christmas dinner. Sharon has got her teeth into a drumstick and keeps giving me this look over it, my opinion is she ought to see a vet. After dinner, there's family games: me and Sharon's brother Syd from New Cross play Double Diamond. I beat him by nine bottles, and we both go upstairs for a bit of a lie down on the bed.

I can hear Sharon yelling faintly, I suppose it must have been about 4 a.m., but I drop off again, thank God.

FRIDAY, DECEMBER 26

Something grabs me and I wake up petrified but it is only Syd. No sign of Sharon. Syd and me go downstairs and have a bit of breakfast, on account of there's still nearly three crates more or less untouched, and we are just going through the bin for any large dog-ends when Sharon comes in. She is wearing an angora sweater about three sizes too small, probably a 42, and a black satin skirt split to the thigh.

You must have caught it on a nail, says Syd and before she's finished chucking bottles at him, I have got my anorak and cap on. A lot of blokes do not get on with their brothers-in-law, but me and Syd, we're like that, and it is not difficult to understand why, he is the salt of the earth and knows which bloody way the wind blows!

Where are you off to now, says Sharon, and her mouth looks like a pair of pliers; football, I reply, me and Syd always go to football, it is one of the oldest South London traditions, Boxing Day football.

Well, how long you be, says Sharon? Hard to say exactly, I reply, this year we're watching Dundee versus Ayr United.

SATURDAY, DECEMBER 27

Swansea.

It was changing at Crewe that buggered it, says Syd, if it *was* Crewe, I suppose it could've been Peterborough, they all look the same from the floor, was Stockport the one where they never had Bass?

No, I reply, you're thinking of Yarmouth. Where the little bloke took his appliance off and those two darkies had a punch-up about *Mastermind*.

Get off, that was Nuneaton, says Syd, I remember it was Nuneaton on account of that little hill outside the station where we had to run after the bottle of Haig, it wasn't half travelling.

The last train back to London come in then. At least, I think it was to London.

I can see where Sharon is a bit choked when she opens the door, on account of she is wearing this pink nylon sort of housecoat thing with like a pink feather boa effort as a collar, and the air is whistling out of her conk so fast all the feathers are lying dead flat; what with her flared nostrils and her rolling eyes and all the rest of it, she looks like a runaway bloody carthorse.

She calms down a bit when she sees the Old Bill, and they explain about how the Fire Brigade had to get me out of this tree Sunday morning near Welshpool, but they are not pressing charges on account of it being the season of goodwill etcetera etcetera. I do not want to point out that it could not have been Sunday because yesterday was Saturday, I do not go around losing whole days, nor does Syd, wherever he is, because I tried informing them of that in the car and they handcuffed me to their bloody Alsatian.

Anyway, as I say, she calms down a bit, and then she says it's all right, officers, I will look after him, and I can see the colour is coming back to her cheeks, and I was not born yesterday, I know that look, it is the way she looked the night I got trapped into what ended up as Eamonn Terry Melvyn, serve me right for coming home sober due to row up Rat & Cockle concerning knocking over a pile of pennies for the lifeboat and so forth. I know what's brought that look on, it is these berks in their uniforms, Sharon is off like a ferret at the sight of a cap-badge; I have got to find a way out of this, so I say: thanks very much lads, come in for a quick one seeing as it is Yuletide, and they do not mind if they do.

TUESDAY, DECEMBER 30

Wake up in bath. Someone is shaking me; it is of course my beloved bleeding Sharon in mail-order baby doll night-dress and lurex suspender-belt, and I can see she is about to get in the bath, and I say bloody hell, not here, can't you see there's a copper asleep on the lav, you can

157

probably get three years just for thinking about it in front of the Filth, so she bangs my head on the taps, and turns on the cold shower, and slams the door, and the copper wakes up, and he says, stone me, you look like you could do with a drink, one good turn, know what I mean, come down the station, we got a bit of a seasonal blast on, draught Guinness, no rubbish, WPC jumping out of a cake, all that.

So we collect his oppo from on top of the fridge, and the Alsation brings me back at midnight.

WEDNESDAY, DECEMBER 31
All right, I say, all right, I give up, I am prepared to see the old year out with a bang, har, har, har! God you're common, she says, which I cannot help thinking is a bit bloody strong coming from her, she is done up in cowboy boots, fishnet tights, a gold lamé peephole bra and a beehive wig in metallic eau-de-nil, and it is half past five in the afternoon.

But anything for a bit of peace and quiet, is my view, and I am just steeling myself with four or five trebles while she is upstairs putting red bulbs in the bedside lamps when the doorbell chimes, and stone me! There on the mat is Big Brian, Jeff, Little Brian, Eric, Kevin, Irish Brian, the Other Jeff, Brian, and Brian's cousin from up north, Brian From Up North!

And they're all yelling HAPPY NEW YEAR HAPPY NEW YEAR, and before I know it, we're all down the old Rat & Cockle and we 're getting them in, and sticking darts in one another, and throwing pickled eggs about, and singing the old songs, and breaking bottles over our heads, and, well, just bloody marvellous, is what it is!

About ten o'clock, Norman the landlord come over and says Sharon is on the phone, and I say Sharon, Sharon, who's Sharon?

Only got one thing on their mind, women.

Lucia di Paddington

An Opera in Three Acts

> ## SINGING IN TRAINS
> ## BANNED IN ITALY

reports the Telegraph. It's still allowed here, though.

ACT ONE: Scene One
Paddington. Before the ticket window. Early evening. A chorus of QUEUERS. To them, enter EDGARDO, running. His tie is under his ear. His umbrella is inside out. There is a dart in his bowler. He runs forward to the booking-clerk, NEXTWINDO.

EDGARDO	Excuse me, is this the –
CHORUS	Oy! Can't you bleeding see? There is a queue!
NEXTWINDO	There is a queue! Can't you bleeding see?
EDGARDO	I'm sorry, I only –
CHORUS	He's sorry! Jumps the queue, bold as you bloody please –
NEXTWINDO	– and says he's sorry! I'll give him sorry!
CHORUS	We'll give him bloody sorry! There is a queue here, sunshine! Not surprising there is a dart stuck in his hat!
EDGARDO	It happened on the Tube, there was this punk –
NEXTWINDO	Not surprising there is a dart stuck in his hat! In my opinion, he is lucky it is not a bloody cleaver!
CHORUS	Jumping queues etcetera, we are surprised it is not a bloody cleaver!

159

EDGARDO	I only want to know if I am right for Pangbourne.
NEXTWINDO	He only wants to know if he is right for bloody Pangbourne! Can he not see I only got one pair of bloody hands?
CHORUS	He cannot see you only got one pair of bloody hands! He cannot see we are a bloody queue. Some people!
NEXTWINDO	Some people! Is it any wonder the country is up the spout?
CHORUS	No, it is no wonder the country is up the spout!

(EDGARDO joins the end of the queue. The queue shuffles forward, coughing over one another unaccompanied, since the orchestra has now been diverted to Taplow, due to a chance of sleet on the points at Didcot. After twenty minutes, EDGARDO reaches the window. The clerk NEXTWINDO puts up a POSITION CLOSED sign, and exit.)

ANNOUNCER	*(off):* Mglgnk wblegnk Pangbngl Readijlgwn Oxfngnd Maidenbgl fmswlb jimgln bumgluk!
EDGARDO	Oh! Was that something about Pangbourne? *(Turns desperately, to find two porters)* Thank God! Could you tell me if –
WHOMEO?	Who me?
WHOHIMO?	Who him?
WHOMEO?	Is this prat addressing me on a matter not germane to portering?
WHOHIMO?	Is this prat addressing you on a matter not germane to portering?
WHOMEO?	He does not realize I have a bad back! He no doubt reckons I am leaning on this trolley for my own bloody amusement!
WHOHIMO?	He no doubt reckons I am lying on these suitcases for a giggle! He does not realize I did my shoulder a mischief last Christmas carrying that woman's bloody chicken!

160

WHOMEO?	Or was it the Christmas before?
WHOHIMO?	Yes, it could have been the Christmas before. Or was that the Christmas you put your back out picking up your fags?
WHOMEO?	It might have been. All I know is I have enough trouble due to these dizzy spells etcetera without sodding about answering questions which do not fall within my agreed sphere of responsibility!
WHOHIMO?	You have *quite* enough trouble due to these dizzy spells etcetera without sodding about answering questions which do not fall within your agreed sphere of responsibility, nor me with my wossname, shoulder!
WHOMEO?	Nor you with your wossname, shoulder!
ANNOUNCER	*(off)*: Svmbl grgl nern nern Pangbldge Readnarngl Oxfumb Maidenglngfnifl rarb hnonk!
EDGARDO	Oh!

(Exeunt)

Scene Two

Pangbourne. A station carpark. Enter twelve VOLVOS. From the first, LUCIA emerges. From the others, a chorus of WIVES.

LUCIA	I hope he is not late, his boss Chairmano is coming to dinner!
CHORUS	His boss Chairmano is coming to dinner! If Edgardo is late, the quiche will be like a brick!
LUCIA	The quiche will be like a brick! The roast pheasant will be the size of a sparrow! And God alone knows what will happen to the crème brûlée!
CHORUS	What will happen to the crème brûlée is you will have to eat it with a chisel!
LUCIA	Woe! Woe!

(Exeunt, bitching)

161

ACT TWO: Scene One

A corridor drawing out of Paddington. Later evening.
Enter EDGARDO. His tie has gone. His umbrella is in
two halves. He slides open a compartment door, to reveal
a chorus of NONSMOKERS. They shriek.

CHORUS
: No smoking! Wurggh! Cancer! Yegh! Bronchitis! Clear off!

EDGARDO
: I am not smoking!

CHORUS
: He says he is not smoking! Pull this one, it has got bells on! We have heard that one before! Let him in here, next thing you know he will be chugging like a bloody steamroller!

EDGARDO
: Oh no, I shall not!

CHORUS
: Oh no, he shall not, and we don't think! Oh no, he shall not, and we should perishing cocoa! Ugh! We shall catch arthritis off him! Faugh! He will give us all wooden legs!

(They slam the door. Edgardo stands in the corridor.
Enter HALLO, a ticket collector.)

HALLO
: Hallo! What is this? Only someone causing an obstruction!

EDGARDO
: I cannot find a seat! Will you not take pity upon me?

HALLO
: Hallo, we have a right one here! It is not my business to find people seats, if I was from the Sally bloody Army I would have a bonnet on!

(The compartment door opens again.)

CHORUS
: He only wanted to come in here and smoke, didn't he?

HALLO
: Hallo! This looks like a further contravention under the Bloodyminded Passengers Act of 1953, as if he was not in enough trouble already!

EDGARDO
: As if I was not in enough trouble already!

CHORUS
: As if he was not in enough trouble already!

(The door slams again. The train slows down.)

HALLO   Hallo! This looks like Westbourne Park!
Yes, I should be surprised if this did not
turn out to be Westbourne Park! I am
prepared to be lenient this time, I shall
not press charges, I shall merely chuck
you off here, do not say I am not a lenient
man, nothing wrong with Westbourne
Park!

(Edgardo is ejected.)

Scene Two

*Pangbourne. Even later evening. An entirely pine
kitchen. DOZIA, an au pair, is watching a saucepan of
leek soup boiling over and fusing itself to the Scholtes
hob. In a corner, a small CHILD is eating a 13-amp plug.
There is a fearful crash without. Enter LUCIA, her hair
in disarray.*

LUCIA   Ayee! Woe! The front wing has demol-
ished our magnolia! A wheel has come
off! Edgardo is nowhere to be found!
Chairmano is imminent! What will
become of me?

DOZIA   Gimme night off. Gimme tights allowance. Gimme large gin.

CHILD   Choke!

(Exeunt)

ACT THREE: Scene One

*Crewe. Night. A buffet. Enter PTOMAINIA, a tea-lady,
and BARBADO, a guard. To them, staggering, EDGAR-
DO. His umbrella has gone. He has one shoe.*

EDGARDO   A cup of tea, for the love of God!

PTOMAINIA   A cup of tea? *A cup of tea?* Where does he
think he is, Claridges?

BARBADO   Where do he think he are, man, damn
Claridges? A cuppa tea!

EDGARDO   I should have been in Pangbourne three

	hours ago! I am dying! What am I doing in Crewe?
BARBADO	What he doin' in Crewe is gittin' on people's wick! Prancin' in here like de famous Earl o' Bostick, demandin' tea at damn ten o'clock!
PTOMAINIA	Demanding bloody tea at ten o'clock! Some people do not realize we close at midnight! Some people do not realize I got a glass to wipe!
BARBADO	Some damn people not appreciatin' where you got a whole damn bun to put back in de dustbin fo' tomorrow! Some damn people not realizin' it necessitatin' a good two hours, puttin' de rat-poison under de cake-stand!

(They switch off the urn. They eat the sandwich. They put out the lights.)

EDGARDO	My God! How am I to get back to Pangbourne?
BARBADO	Now he yellin' about gittin' back to damn Pangbourne!
PTOMAINIA	Disturbing everyone, screaming about getting back to bloody Pangbourne! Some people do not appreciate that there is no way of returning to Pangbourne after ten pee em!
BARBADO	Ain't no way anyone gittin' back to Pangbourne, man!
EDGARDO	Woe!
BARBADO	Unless de Footer Special stoppin' here on de way back from Manchester, to drop off de corpses!

(BARBADO and PTOMAINIA exeunt boogying. EDGARDO falls down and, crawling, exit. Sound of train-brakes, off. Rattles, shrieks, chants, grenades.)

Scene Two
(Pangbourne. After midnight. CHAIRMANO and his

164

wife ANOREXIA sit staring at a small charred thing,
formerly a pheasant, by guttering candlelight. Beneath
the table, DOZIA and GRANADO, a TV repairman, are
putting their clothes back on.)

CHAIRMANO   This will cost him the South East Area
Divisional Sales Managership, you mark
my words!

ANOREXIA   I mark your words, Chairmano, and I
trust his new position will not carry a
company car?

CHAIRMANO   You trust correctly, his new position will
carry a company broom! I do not know
what young people today are coming to!

ANOREXIA   What are young people today coming to?
Personally, I do not believe this young
man is repairing the au pair, as he claims,
do you, Chairmano?

CHAIRMANO   No, if you want my honest opinion, I –

(Enter LUCIA. Her eyes roll in her head, she staggers as
one inebriated, she plucks at her clothing. She bangs her
head on the wall.)

ANOREXIA   She has gone mad!

CHAIRMANO   And I have had no pudding! It is not
typical of young people today, to get up
from dinner and go mad?

ANOREXIA   Without so much as by your leave! To go
mad and not even put the percolator on!

LUCIA   I have gone mad, but can you blame me?
Let me switch on the floodlighting and
show you what is standing in the pond
next to our heron!

CHAIRMANO   My God, it is Edgardo!

ANOREXIA   Can that possibly be Edgardo?

LUCIA   Yes, I may be off my trolley, but even I can
recognize Edgardo!

(EDGARDO stands in the pond, naked but for a Chelsea
scarf. He carries a lavatory pan, an empty Ruddles firkin,
and, beneath his arm, a carriage door. He has no teeth,
but he is laughing, noiselessly. As they watch, a BR

lightbulb falls out of his ear and explodes on the heron's
beak. In the far distance, a train whistle blows.)

CURTAIN

The Curious Case of the Distressed Gentlefolk

Shares are being offered for sale in the house in which Sir Arthur Conan Doyle set his story, *The Hound of the Baskervilles*.

A London-based property company is turning the house, Clyro Court, at Hay-on-Wye, in Wales, into a time-sharing holiday home. For £500 a thousand people will be able to take a week's holiday there for the next 40 years and enjoy the prestige that part-owning the house brings.

The Times

I stood gloomily at the cobwebbed window of 221B Baker Street, gazing out at the impenetrable yellow fog and gnawing upon the tasteless shin of some small and unidentifiable animal whose bold claim to have been fried in Kentucky had been rendered irrelevant by the appalling things which must subsequently have happened to it on the long voyage over.

That my illustrious friend and I were subject to such dismal fare was entirely due to the grotesque venality of our housekeeper Mrs Hudson, who, such are the fearful times in which we now live, had not only, a month before, demanded a wage-increase far in excess of the guidelines laid down by Her Majesty's troubled Government, but had also, upon being dismissed, immediately dragged us before an industrial tribunal who had seen fit to uphold her claim for unfair dismissal and set so preposterous a sum for compensation that Holmes and I were plunged into a penury yet worse than any we had hitherto experienced in these recessive times.

My melancholy reflections were broken by an oath behind me. I turned. Sherlock Holmes, who had been perusing the newspaper with his customary assiduousness, now flung it aside furiously.

'What is it, Holmes?' I cried. 'Have the plans of the new torpedo been snatched from beneath the very noses of our trusty curators of the Queen's pictures? Have our American cousins exploded a thermonuclear device on County Hall to indicate their concern at a dangerously left-wing transport policy? Has Sir Keith Moriarty escaped from his locked cupboard in the Cabinet Room?'

Holmes shook his angular head impatiently.

'Wrong as ever, Watson,' he muttered. 'It is far worse than that. For the twelfth day running, the numbers upon our Bingo card have failed utterly to tally with those in the morning's paper! How can this be? These are deep waters, Watson.'

He hurled himself into our one remaining armchair and, his Stradivarius having long departed in the interests of our supplementary rates demand, snatched up a battered kazoo upon which he managed a few pitiful bars of *Darktown Strutters Ball*, before his spittle dried.

He stared up at me, hollow-eyed – though not, I knew, from drugs, these now lying so far beyond his pocket that my poor friend had been reduced to sucking Elastoplast in the vain hope that some minuscule narcotic might thence be gleaned.

'I confess I know not where to turn, old Watson,' he muttered. 'The recession has sunk its fangs so deep that potential clients cannot even afford to insert items in the personal columns of *The Times*, let alone command our services, and as for the current rate for inland telegrams –'

Prophetic word! For, hardly had it left his emaciated lip, than there came a thunderous pounding upon our door. Holmes snatched the envelope, ripped it open, smote his forehead, laughed aloud, and handed it to me.

'At last, Watson!' he cried, much in the manner of his old self. 'A case meet for our talents!'

I looked at the telegram; the message was terse.

'COME AT ONCE TO BASKERVILLE HALL. I KNOW NOT WHERE TO TURN.'

'Baskerville Hall!' exclaimed Holmes. 'I do believe, old friend, that things are looking up, at last!'

And, pausing only at our corner pawnbroker's to hock our toaster in order to redeem Holmes's deerstalker, we made our hurried way to Paddington.

It was many years since Sherlock Holmes and I had visited the teetering pile of Baskerville Hall, and we were thus ill-prepared for the changes which had been wrought upon it: it was not merely the miniature golf-course, most of whose hazards involved the well-endowed anatomy of large plaster females, which caught our attention, nor the safari park dotted with elderly okapi, nor even the West Wing Casino which connected with the East Wing Roller-Disco by means of the Minstrels' Strip 'n' Mature-Video Gallery, so much as the figure of Sir Henry Baskerville himself who struggled down the gravelled path to meet us.

He was clad in the green cloth head of Kermit the Frog, and tugging a leash attached to a mildewed and malodorous camel, from the hump of which three extraordinary young people with orange hair and glue-tubes depending from their safety-pinned nostrils were pelting him with individual fruit pies.

Seeing us, he dropped the leash, and ran forward, two huge tears spilling from his rheumy eyes and spreading darkly upon the verdant fabric of his cheeks.

'Holmes!' he cried, 'Watson! My dear, dear friends –' he paused, he caught a sob, he spread mute hands to indicate the dreadfulness that lay to right and left '– that it should all have come to this!'

Holmes stayed his sorrowful flow with a firm, yet not unkindly, hand.

'Let us not refer to it again, Sir Henry,' he declared roundly. 'It is a story that may be replicated among many of our acquaintance. Why, we ourselves have experienced the odd vicissitude, have we not, doctor?'

'One can, with practice, grow quite fond of Whiskas,' I replied.

'Good old Watson!' cried Holmes. 'You are the one fixed point in a changing age.' His smile disappeared, to be replaced with a grimness of the lip and a darkness of the brow as he turned again to Baskerville. 'But we delay. Your telegram, Sir Henry, indicated some urgency, I believe?'

The old gentleman drew off his batrachian head and cast it aside.

'Follow me,' he muttered.

We did so, entering Baskerville Hall via the Space Invaders suite and rapidly proceeding thence to the upper apartments. There seemed to be several of these to a corridor, each with a differently coloured door and a distinguishing title beneath its bronzette carriage-lamp – *Benidorm*, *Erzanmine*, *Duncarin*, *Crossroads*, and so on. Before a puce door marked *Arsenal*, Sir Henry stopped, and pressed the bell.

Hardly had the chimes of *You'll Never Walk Alone* died away than a small woman in obvious distress appeared in the doorway. Behind her stood a thin balding man, soaked to the skin.

'Yes?' snapped the man irritably. 'What is it? We're up to here with wossname.'

'So I can see,' replied Holmes curtly. 'But, apart from the obvious facts that you are a tobacconist, a cheese-label collector, a Woolwich investor, a teetotaller, an insomniac, a Presbyterian, a mason, and a childhood sufferer from projectile vomiting, I know nothing whatever about you. However, if you will allow me to enter and –'

''Ere,' cried the man, 'he's from the bleeding VAT!'

He made as if to slam the door, but Baskerville quickly forestalled him.

'This,' he announced, 'is Mr Sherlock Holmes!'

The man's scowl vanished, his wife clasped her hands and fell to her knees.

'Sherlock Holmes!' she cried. 'Thank God you've come!'

'No time for that, madame!' snapped Holmes. 'Be so good as to give me the salient details as quickly and as cogently as you are able.'

170

In answer, the thin man pointed to his saturated clothes.

'It is our low-flush avocado cistern, Mr 'Olmes,' he said. 'It has been like this for three days!'

'The cistern?' shouted Holmes, ripping off his overcoat. 'Quick, Watson, there is not a moment to lose! Pray God that we are not too late!'

With one bound, Holmes sprang across the living room, hurled wide two intervening doors and, with that uncanny knack of his, found himself in the bathroom. Close behind him, I had not been prepared for the fearful sight that met our eyes. In all my wide experience at the side of Holmes, I had never seen such appalling devastation: the water was knee-deep, sodden towels lay everywhere, a matching bathmat and seat-cover had shrunk to sickening proportions, and in the scummy tide, plastic ducks and smart souvenirs bobbed pitifully. I particularly noticed an attractive toothbrush-holder in the shape of a toreador with a space between his legs for the easy withdrawal of dental floss, now warped almost beyond recognition.

'Dear Heavens, Holmes,' I muttered, averting my eyes. 'Can all of this be the work of our old adversary, the ball-cock?'

'I fear it is far worse than that, Watson,' snapped Holmes. He flung aside a marbletto-tiled panel with deceptive strength and stared at the tangled plumbing behind. 'As I thought,' he cried, 'this is a three-pipe problem! Watson, do you have your service spanner?'

I drew my old Stilson from my dungaree pocket and handed it to him. His upper body disappeared into the dreadful cavity.

'We have not yet met our Waterloo, Watson,' came back his muffled voice, 'but this is our Marengo!'

For some time, while I (and all the world, it seemed) scarce dared draw breath, Sherlock Holmes threw himself into that fearful struggle. I cannot tell how long it was before my brave friend finally emerged from that black hole, his face flushed beneath the filth, but

171

smiling, and flung the wrench aside.

'There!' he cried. 'It was as I had suspected, Watson, all along – at some time during the recent conversion operations, an unskilled hand had attempted to marry a $^{11}/_{16}$ brass union with an $^9/_{16}$ inlet conduit, thereby creating a backflow beyond the capacity of the Norland valve. It was the work of a moment to deduce that the resulting distortion to the plunger-cowl lay at the very heart of our problem.'

'Amazing!' I exclaimed.

'Elementary,' said Holmes.

'But whoever would have thought that an overloaded Norland valve –'

Holmes held up a grimy hand and fixed me with his sternest eye.

'How often have I said to you, Watson, that when you have eliminated the impossible, whatever remains, *however improbable*, must be the truth?' His face relented. 'Finish up here, old friend, will you?'

It remained only for me to rebraze the union and give it a cursory wipe with my trusty moleskin, and our task was done. We returned to the living room and our clients' gratitude, less ten per cent discount for cash.

Sir Henry Baskerville himself accompanied us down the gravel path once more, by now dressed, for his Kiddies' Teatime role, as a giant donut.

'I cannot thank you enough, Mr Holmes,' he said. 'The official plumbers were baffled.'

Holmes gave a wintry smile.

'They usually are,' he murmured. 'The old skills, my dear Baskerville, are vanishing, much like the old ways.'

Sir Henry glanced from the desecration of his beautiful house to the bag of tools I carried in my hand, and sighed.

'That you and I,' he said softly, 'should have come to this.'

Holmes shrugged.

'If one insists upon living to a hundred and thirty,' he said, 'one must be prepared to accept the consequences.'

Zuleika Capp

'No sex' shock by students

MALE students at a top college have put soccer telly and tradition before the chance to live with girls.

They fear nights of watching programmes like Match of the Day, will come to an end if the girls move into their halls of residence.

The Sun

That old bell, presage of a train, had just sounded through Oxford station; and the undergraduates who were waiting there moved to the margin of the platform and gazed idly up the line. Young and careless, in the glow of the afternoon sunshine, they struck a sharp note of incongruity with the worn boards they stood on, with the grey eternal walls of that antique station, which whisper to the tourist the last enchantments of the Middle Age.

At the door of the waiting-room stood the Warden of Judas, a pillar of tradition, the falsetto stanchion of a hundred _Any Questions?_, the gargling link-man of his own 26-part BBC-2 series _Mankind In A Nutshell_, as frequent a Parkinson guest as he was a Mustique visitor, a man who had played Juliet to Eric Morecambe's Romeo and Lord Falkender to a thousand publishers' parties, and was to go by the code-name Judy Garland in the imminent Blunt memoirs; he was, _en bref_, the very model of a modern academic.

Came a honk from the distance. The rails sang. The

breast of a diesel was descried, and a long train curving after it. It grew and grew, it hummed into the station, its brakes howled, and ere it had yet stopped, the door of one carriage flew open, and from it, her electric blue Zandra Rhodes one-off a-billow, her tiny nostril secured by the most discreet of garnet brooches, a lithe and radiant creature slipped nimbly down to the platform.

'Zuleika!' shrilled the Warden.

'Grandpa!' trilled the vision.

Yet, ere the two could engage their embrace, the massed undergraduates, unable longer to contain themselves, surged forward. The other doors burst open, and from them, screaming, poured five hundred flailing blue-scarved figures. The undergraduates plunged into them! Knees met groins, elbows impaled eyes, teeth flew thick as oaths, skulls drove into cigarette-machines, until, as the railway police and their trusty Dobermanns lashed out with fang and truncheon, the whole boiling mass stormed, howling, from the ruined station.

The Warden picked Zuleika up. Her dress was shredded, her heels were amputated, her lovely eyelashes were pitifully ungummed. The Warden gazed at her disembowelled Gucci luggage, and shook his head sadly.

'It's always the same,' he said, 'when Millwall play Oxford United.'

The warm bells tolled over evening Oxford, speaking each to each, shaking, it seemed, the lengthening shadows across Judas Quad.

It was the Newcastle Brown hour.

In thirty ancient butteries, the undergraduates were falling down the steps and, at the worn oak tables, throwing up over their Littlewoods coupons. But in the Warden's lodgings, all was calm. Zuleika, bathed and recoiffed, was sipping a bourbon sour, across the frosted rim of which she smiled, now, at her grandpapa as he dictated the last paragraph of his learned paper, *Mugabe the Coconut Hitler!*, to his lissome secretary, Gerald.

174

'Wonderful!' cried Zuleika. 'What is it for?'

'A fiver a word,' replied the Warden, 'isn't it, Gerald?'

'Yes, dear,' said the secretary, and slipped away to telephone the *Sunday Express*.

'I've organized a little dinner party to celebrate your arrival,' said the Warden. 'Just a few young people of your own age, the Duke of Dorset, Viscount Hambledon, the Marquis of Flint, Kevin Noaks.'

'Kevin Noaks!' exclaimed Zuleika, clapping her lovely hands. 'Isn't his father Bolshie Noaks, the international picketing star?'

'He is, indeed,' replied the Warden. 'It was at his intercession that Judas agreed to give young Noaks a scholarship, despite the fact that he had only one CSE and that the University had, at that time, no Faculty of Corner-Kicking, the one discipline at which the boy excelled. But his father came to me and explained that if we did not provide his son with the facilities which were his democratic right, then the NUM would dig up Judas and the T&GWU would take it away in trucks.'

The door opened, knocking over the butler, and the four young men came into the room.

'Gentlemen,' said the Warden, 'may I present my grand-daughter Zuleika?'

Zuleika, her china-blue eyes wide and sparkling, smiled ravishingly.

'We give it to 'em on a bleeding plate,' said the Duke of Dorset.

'Calls hisself a striker,' shouted Viscount Hambledon, 'he wouldn't get past Long John bloody Silver without a bicycle!'

'Good evening,' said Zuleika.

'Sick as a parrot,' said Noaks. 'What am I?'

'Sick as a parrot,' said the Marquis of Flint. He spat in the wastebin.

The butler, who had meanwhile crawled out, now returned.

'Dinner is served,' he announced.

He took six alloy trays from his trolley, and handed

175

them round. The undergraduates drew their chairs up in a ring around the television set, switched it on, and began shovelling Vesta prawn curry somewhat erratically into their mouths.

'Clever bugger, Jimmy Saville,' said the Marquis of Flint, 'learning all that stuff by heart.'

'Gerroff!' cried the Duke of Dorset, removing a prawn from his nose. 'They write it on a wossname, lens. All he's got to do is read it.'

'Even so,' said Viscount Hambledon. 'Some of them words got syllables all over 'em.'

'I can't stand the bastard,' said Noakes savagely. Rice flecked the screen. 'I only wrote into *Jim'll Fix It* three months back, didn't I? Has he replied yet? Has he hell!'

'What did you ask him to fix?' enquired the Marquis.

'I wanted to punch Charlie George in the mouth,' replied Noaks.

In the darkening corner, a tear ran gently down Zuleika's cheek, catching the starlight.

It was the morrow morn, the spring sun twinkling off the ancient stone, as Zuleika limped down the Broad. Despite the sliding tackle with which three under-graduates, dribbling out of Balliol, had felled her, laddering her tights and bringing an unfamiliar throb to her left ear, her spirits were high as she turned through the Judas gate. For had not Kevin Noaks himself, as the porters bore him singing from the Warden's lodging last midnight, invited her to a party in his room?

Would there, she asked herself, as she climbed the staircase, be plovers' eggs and glinting caviar in beds of ice, would there be Dom Perignon, or perhaps Bucks Fizz, would there be Albinoni on the gramophone and slim men in the sun-drenched window-seats, reading aloud imperishable sonnets of which the ink was not yet dry?

'Come!' cried a voice, as she tapped the antique oak. She walked in.

176

'Your two quid,' coughed Noaks, through a bobbing millimetre of Woodbine, 'and up two.'

The four young brag-players sat in their vests around a Morris Motors packing case, its ancient edge charred from a thousand stubs. It had belonged to Kevin Noaks's father, and to his father before him; from factory to factory they had borne it, a living piece of British industrial history. There was saw-dust on the floor, and a hundred ring-pulls, and fifty nude calendars upon the walls, the darts hurled into them with such unerring accuracy that Zuleika winced, and felt faint.

'Good morning,' she said.

'It's all over there,' said Kevin, nodding, not taking his eyes from the cards, particularly those of the youth next to him.

Zuleika glanced towards the corner. Two sliced loaves stood upon a table, next to a plate of fly-specked ham, a greasy brick of well-thumbed cheddar, a can of sardines, a jar of pickled onions, a dish of butter with a sock over it to keep off the sun, and an open tin of luncheon-meat with a jam-spoon embedded in it.

'Ah,' said Zuleika, 'one helps oneself, does one?'

Four pairs of eyes lifted, at last, from the cards.

'Stone me!' said the Duke of Dorset.

'Bloody stroll on!' cried the Marquis of Flint.

'One is looking for a poke in the gob,' said Viscount Hambledon, 'from the sound of it.'

'Leave it out,' grunted Noaks. 'She's a guest. Look, love,' he said, 'it's two ham for me, pickled onions on one, sliced thin, one cheese, no onions; one sardine for Flint –'

'And mind you take the spines out,' interrupted the Marquis, 'one thing you don't want in a sardine sarny is nothing crunchy, am I right?'

'Right!' snapped the Duke of Dorset. 'And I like ham *with* cheese, no onion, twice. I'll see you for five,' he added.

'Three luncheon meat for me,' said Viscount Hambledon, 'and pick out the gristle. I got three tens,' he

177

continued, drawing the pot towards him. He selected three notes therefrom, and held them out to the trembling Zuleika.

'Here you go, gel,' he said. 'When you've done the sandwiches, nip down the off-licence, pick us up a crate of Worthington.'

Zuleika, however, did not wait. Her lovely eyes welling with tears, she stumbled from the room, clattered down the staircase, and ran, sobbing, from the hallowed portals of Judas College.

'Funny cow,' said Noaks. 'I got three kings.'

Those who had known the beautiful Zuleika during her short and brittle life would not, perhaps, have been surprised to see her now, standing upon the parapet of Folly Bridge. For it had been a life marked by the disappointments of the heart and sustained only by the search for love. She had, it is true, known Kevin Noaks but a scant dozen hours, yet it had been enough for her to recognize that, for her, no other paramour would suffice, and that no other course, upon his rejection, lay open but the present one.

At the terrible sound of the splash, two elegant Christ Church men, who had been practising penalty shots on the towpath, ran quickly to the river bank and peered down into the swirling torrent.

After a few seconds, holding wet fingers to the wind and such, they shaded their eyes to watch the river bear away its tragic burden.

'I reckon she'll get to Iffley Lock in half an hour,' said one.

The other shook his head.

'With this wind,' he said, 'twenty minutes, top whack.'

'Two quid?' said the first.

'You're on!' cried the second.

They grabbed their bicycles, and pedalled quickly off.

Going Like a Bomb

Free nuclear fall-out shelters are being offered by Penta Garage, Reading, with all £18,000 Jaguar XJ12s ordered from stock before August 1. – Daily Telegraph

It was August 1.

'Well?' said the man. 'Do I know a bargain, or do I know a bargain?'

He walked, slowly, around the car again. In the twenty-four hours since he had bought it, he had made some fifty of these rapt circumambulations. It was the furthest he had ever walked in a day.

'It was worth,' he said confidently, giving the brightwork an umpteenth buff, 'waiting for black. They said: We could do you a magenta right now, cream coachline, dove-grey hide; very chic, magenta. I looked them in the eye. Know what I said? Sod that, I said. I could tell they were impressed. The thing is, when you have built a gravel pit company up from nothing, I mean bloody *nothing*, until you are nationally recognized as one of the country's leading grit concerns, thirty trucks, no rubbish, offices done out *entirely* in teak, when you have done *that*, people don't mess you about. They take one look, and they *know*, follow my meaning?'

The car said nothing.

'Ten a penny, magenta Jags. I might as well have a bronze-bloody-metallic Rover, I said, I might as well have a lime Audi. I am after, I said, something distinguished, something you can pull up in outside the Playboy Club and people turn round.'

He walked to the end of the shelter, turned at the lead-lined door, and squinted happily down the shimmering length of bonnet.

'The body,' he said, to a head-high stack of tinned food, 'the body is completely submersed in a rust-inhibiting solution what penetrates every crevice and seam. After that, they put on ten coats. *And*,' he added, tapping the stack with a manicured forefinger, 'they inject it with cavity-protecting wax.'

He got in, sank into the fawn hide, touched a finger to the saddle-stitching, shut the door.

'Hear that clunk?' he cried, as his window sighed electrically down, to his deep-freeze. 'Hear that clunk? That is not bodywork, son, that is *coach*work!' He glanced at the dashboard clock. 'Eighteen hours,' he murmured. 'Must be all right by now. Quick spin can't hurt, keep the windows up, put the air-conditioning on.'

He got out again, and opened the shelter door.

'Stone me!' he said.

The house had gone. The staircase remained, connecting with nothing, but the house had gone.

'A hundred grand,' he told the car bitterly. 'And do they insure you against acts of war? Do they buggery! Still,' he said, as he climbed back behind the wheel, 'it's a bloody good shelter. I was definitely not done over the shelter. All I heard last night was a bit of a rumble. Free shelter stands up, hundred bloody grand house falls down, sunnink wrong there, am I right?' The steering-wheel did not reply. 'Time I've finished with that builder, he'll be lucky to get a job selling Lego.'

He switched on the ignition: twelve pistons moved silently inside the aluminium block; the GM 400 automatic gearbox engaged imperceptibly. Gently, the man eased the car forward.

'Smooth,' he murmured, 'but strong.'

The car rolled down the pitted drive, and turned onto the rubbled road, without a lurch. The man beamed.

'Incredible!' he cried. 'That is what I *call* anti-drive geometry, that is what I *call* independent suspension, being able to drive on a road what has sustained a major thermo-bloody-nuclear attack and not feel *nothing!* It is like driving across a billiard table,' he informed the seat beside him. 'It is *magic!*'

He drove the eight miles into Maidenhead, but it wasn't there.

'Good job I got a full tank,' he said, passing a scorch above which the twisted BP sign hung uncertainly, and turned onto the M4, towards London. 'Pity about Maidenhead,' he said to the cigar-lighter, 'I fancied tonking past old Charlie Bassett's place, he's always out front admiring his Mercedes. Or was. Don't talk to me about Mercedes, I could give him two seconds start and still see him off over the kilometre, this is five litres we're talking about!' And here he punched his foot into the floor, so that the car hurled itself forward down the empty fast lane. It had reached a hundred before he knew it. His heart sang! It was the Goodwood Straight, it was Druid's, it was the chicanes at Woodcote, and Mario Andretti was half a lap behind, trailing his dust.

'Bugger!' he cried.

He had passed the police car at a hundred and twenty. It lurked on the hard shoulder, the way they always did. He hit the brakes, the pads closed on the spinning discs, the car decelerated; but not, he knew, enough to kid them. He looked fatalistically in his mirror.

The police car had not moved.

'My lucky day,' said the man, lifting his foot from the brake.

He passed a lot of cars after that; but none of them moved. Galling. There was no other word for it. There were magenta Jags, Rolls-Royces, BMWs, he could have left them *standing!* As, of course, he did. There was even a Ferrari, just past Slough, but it was flattened against a flyover pier, and did not therefore offer a significant challenge.

It irked him. He had come a long way to this, shifted a lot of gravel, used up a lot of years, taken a lot of stick from the rich and the flash, and it was his turn, now. But London would be all right, it was not possible to wipe

181

out London, there would be eyes and gasps in London; and women. Fifty wasn't old, they liked grey temples, remember Stewart Granger, and you didn't pay three hundred quid for a suit that didn't disguise your paunch; a black Jag, eight different credit cards, there wasn't a bird alive who wouldn't jump at the Connaught and a tumble at the Ritz.

He came over the Hammersmith Flyover at ninety, whistling *Margie*, and when he pulled up at the first set of lights, there was a Lotus already waiting. He slid alongside, hummed his window down.

'Twenty-two minutes from bloody Maidenhead!' he shouted at the man behind the wheel. 'They don't hang about, these!'

The lights went green, and he flung himself away, leaving tread, laughing. But the challenge went unaccepted. The Lotus dwindled in the mirror, as the lights went red again above it.

Kensington was remarkably intact, all things considered, though full of bodies. Once, at the corner of Abingdon Road, he thought he saw a girl with whom the afternoon would be far from wasted; she was standing against a pillar-box and dressed only in the bottom half of a blue bikini, and his temple throbbed as he began to brake. But she turned out to be a model blown across the road from a boutique opposite and fused against the box by her melted plastic; a quirk of the blast.

The Albert Hall fell in as he cruised past; a pity, that. He had always enjoyed wrestling.

He drove around the West End for a while, but there was nothing moving, save the odd tumbling cornice, the odd whirl of dust. In Berkeley Square, he stopped, briefly, outside the Rolls-Royce showrooms, and got out. The plate-glass windows had gone, but the two Corniches within were unblemished. He could, he realized, have simply driven one away, left the Jag there; he could have driven *both* away, black drophead for weekdays, white drophead for weekends. The keys would have been in a drawer, somewhere.

He stepped inside.

'Rolls-Royces!' he shouted. It was more of a scream, really. '*Rolls-Royces!* I wouldn't give you a bloody thank-you for Rolls-Royces! I wouldn't have *four* Rolls-Royces, free! Slow, flash, uneconomical – that's an *old man's* car, that's an *Arab's* car, that's what that is, mate, that's what that bloody is!' He spun on his heel, pointed outside. 'That's what *I* call a car, V-12 configuration, open-deck alloy block with slip-fit cast-iron liners, limited-slip differential, 0–60 in seven bloody seconds, 140 in top, that is what motoring is all about, my son!'

The desks did not reply. The filing cabinets reserved their judgement. The display stands were unmoved.

He wiped his lips with the back of his hand, and, trembling, stepped outside again. The sky was brown.

'I'm the last man in the world,' he said quietly.

At which moment, far off, he heard a squeal of tyres, and the boom of a pedigree engine.

It is not easy to locate a fast-moving noise in the intricated streets of Central London. The man drove the Jaguar, with the windows down and his head poked out, back and forth across the illogical network, and sometimes he lost the other car, and sometimes he found it again, and because it had not chosen to move out of the area, he could only assume that it had heard him, and was searching, too, but he saw nothing. Until, an hour later, soaked with panic and despair, he suddenly turned, almost on a whim, onto Chelsea Embankment, and peered east. The other car, a mile away, was driving west.

Whether from natural fatigue or unnatural infection, his dizziness was no match for his joyful velocity. The impact speed of the two cars, in fact, was close to three hundred miles per hour, which may very well be a record. Which Jaguar was the black and which the magenta, however, it was subsequently impossible to determine.

183

A SELECTION OF BESTSELLERS FROM *SPHERE*

FICTION
A PERFECT STRANGER	Danielle Steel	£1.75 ☐
MISSING PERSONS	C. Terry Cline Jr	£1.95 ☐
A GREEN DESIRE	Anton Myrer	£2.50 ☐
FLOODTIDE	Suzanne Goodwin	£1.95 ☐
JADE TIGER	Craig Thomas	£2.25 ☐

FILM & TV TIE-INS
THE YEAR OF LIVING DANGEROUSLY	C. J. Koch	£1.75 ☐
STAR WARS	George Lucas	£1.75 ☐
FAME	Leonore Fleischer	£1.75 ☐
UPSTAIRS, DOWNSTAIRS	John Hawkesworth	£1.50 ☐

NON-FICTION
A QUESTION OF BALANCE	H.R.H. The Duke of Edinburgh	£1.50 ☐
THE DEATH OF THE DIAMOND	Edward Jay Epstein	£1.95 ☐
SUSAN'S STORY	Susan Hampshire	£1.75 ☐
SECOND LIFE	Stephani Cook	£1.95 ☐
YOU CAN TEACH YOUR CHILD INTELLIGENCE	David Lewis	£1.95 ☐

All Sphere books are available at your local bookshop or newsagent, or can be ordered direct from the publisher. Just tick the titles you want and fill in the form below.

Name _____

Address _____

_____

Write to Sphere Books, Cash Sales Department, P.O. Box 11, Falmouth, Cornwall TR10 9EN

Please enclose cheque or postal order to the value of the cover price plus:

UK: 45p for the first book, 20p for the second and 14p per copy for each additional book ordered to a maximum charge of £1.63.

OVERSEAS: 75p for the first book and 21p for each additional book.

BFPO & EIRE: 45p for the first book, 20p for the second book plus 14p per copy for the next 7 books, thereafter 8p per book.

Sphere Books reserve the right to show new retail prices on covers which may differ from those previously advertised in the text or elsewhere, and to increase postal rates in accordance with the PO.